God's Plan for Church Planting
Church Planting Manual

"This training manual has been a turning point in my ministry. After getting to know and understand what God wants from me as a church planter, I now follow the plan of God. He is building His church today from district to state and from state to another country. I recommend all church planters to know the plan of God for building His church. This manual can help you discover that plan."

—Santosh Makal, Church Planter, West Bengal, India, and Bangladesh

"Your manual is clear, complete, and useful. We train church planters in Ho Chi Minh City with this manual."

—Pastor and Church Planter, Vietnam

"God has used [this manual] to change my life and given the men around me a deep root in the Scriptures. Our church is acting more like the one that the Scriptures talk about and many are blessed because of it."

—Ken Auer, Businessman and Pastor, Raleigh, North Carolina

"I can now say this is next to the Bible in relation to the church and its ministry. You ask how and why? I say, 'Because it takes the reader to the Bible itself to discover the super-cultural, timeless and biblical principles in establishing new churches.' This manual is a tool God can use to empower you to discover the process God wants you to follow."

—Pastor and Church Planter, Myanmar

"The last ten years, I studied and applied this biblical philosophy in my life and ministry. When I studied and used this manual in the ministry, I went from an educator to biblical church planter."

—Mari Daniel, Church Planter, Karnataka, India

"By the end of the book each participant will have his own Bible-based, church planting strategy. The training method used to teach with this manual is very simple. Each question presented makes the participants rely on the Holy Spirit and answer in truth form the Bible. The best thing about the manual is it is very practical."

—Ramesh Sapkota, Church Planter, Former Attorney, Nepal

"Participants who work simultaneously through this training resource are most likely to discover God's biblical strategy for church planting as well as their individual direction for planting churches."

—Phil Largent, President, IMD International, Denver, Colorado

God's Plan
for
Church Planting

Church Planting Manual

**Using God's Timeless,
Supra-Cultural Principles**

Revised Edition

Tim W. Bunn

Westminster, Colorado, USA

God's Plan for Church Planting
Revised Edition

Copyright © 2005, 2008 by IMD Press

Please send requests for information through our website:
www.imdpress.com

ISBN-9: 0-9788201-5-0

ISBN-13: 978-0-9788201-5-2

Printed in the United States of America

Published by IMD Press
7140 Hooker Street
Westminster, CO 80030
www.imdpress.com

Acknowledgments

I have developed this church planting manual to be used for the glory of our Lord and Savior, Jesus Christ! I am grateful for many church leaders who have been blessed by the previous edition as well as the many translations of the Church Planting Manual used throughout the world. I am thankful the revenue from this edition will allow further translations in Asia. To God be the glory!

Since I have been influenced over years of ministry by great men of God, similarities to some of their materials may occur herein. I may have inadvertently used the material of others, but do not wish in any way to take away from the original author nor take credit for any such material. Wherever possible, I have credited those sources.

I would like to offer special recognition to two people who have influenced me greatly in the formation of my philosophy of Church Planting which obviously comes through in this manual. My heartfelt appreciation to Allen Roland of Missionary Methods and Gene Getz, Pastor of Fellowship Bible Church North.

Forward

Over the last three years, I have watched as God linked spiritually ready indigenous leaders with this training manual. The result in almost every such situation is a request to bring the training found in this manual to the ministry in the field. Humbly, we have watched and participated with the Lord in seeing multiple language editions of this manual placed into the hands and lives of key ministry leaders in several countries (the majority in the 10/40 window of South Asia).

Tim Bunn has been captured by the Spirit of God and brought to develop this training manual out of two decades of biblically based, multi-cultural ministry. What you have in hand has been in use (though in earlier forms) for over a decade by indigenous ministry leaders in Asia and South America. It is in use in the USA as well. Thus, the contents of this manual are not theoretical, but practical. God brought these principles to Tim who in turn has released them to leaders throughout the world.

It is clearly the intention of Tim and IMD International that you learn and understand what is presented in this manual as well as implement the same in your ministry. Let God lead you in applying the truths He brings to you through the use of this manual. He only is the **source** and **power** for building His church and expanding it to include all peoples around His earth.

Since "faith comes by hearing and hearing by the Word of God," you can proceed with great faith in studying and applying the truths you will discover through the use of this manual. How can such a strong statement be made concerning faith? Because you are going to be led to open the Bible and let God show you Himself what He has to say about planting churches. Thus, faith in God will be the sure outcome of your study and the certain experience you have with God as you apply what He reveals to you in planting churches.

Surrender your all to the Lord. Apply yourself to completing all the lessons and projects in this manual. Interact with other disciples of Jesus as you walk through these lessons and projects. Plant churches according to His plan in the power of His Spirit. For herein, God is glorified.

A fellow servant of the Lord Jesus Christ and witness to these things,

Phil Largent, IMD International

Contents

Introduction

This manual is a complete tool to guide anointed believers who desire to plant a church (see page 36 for a definition of church planting). It is not training for ministry, rather a training *in* ministry for those who sense God's call.

If you sense this call, you may think that you need a Bible Seminary degree and lots of money to establish a growing church. But the Bible gives us a wonderful example of how the church originally began and spread without degrees or money. By following this example, and with God's blessing, you can be a successful church planter.

Following these lessons will lead you to follow Paul's biblical example of laying the foundation and establishing growing communities of believers. This manual will lead you to develop a church planting strategy of your own, following timeless and supra-cultural biblical principles which are simple, clear, and practical.

'Kingdom gain' is the desired outcome of the time you spend in this manual. To maximize your efforts in learning through the use of this manual, we offer you these important words of encouragement:

- Ask God to give you two or more partners in ministry with whom you can walk together through these learning exercises.

- Intercede one for another constantly as you work through this training manual.

- Read, meditate, and complete every lesson in *God's Plan for Church Planting*. A useful Progress Record (pages 156–159) helps you keep track of your work.

- Dialog with your ministry partners at close or regular intervals as you each work through this manual: listening to one another, praying with one another, and sharing with one another what God is saying to you.

- Trust God for the boldness to accept what He is showing you and for the courage to act upon what He is showing you.

- Apply promptly whatever truths God brings to you as you work through these lessons. Avoid postponing what God leads you to do.

- Ask God to allow you to see more of His plans for your obedience in planting churches—near and far—for His glory.

- Pass on to other disciples of Jesus the truths God is bringing to you through your meditation and application of His Word.

As you look to the Lord, be assured He desires to meet you, raise you up, further equip you, and empower you to plant churches for His glory in your people group and people groups beyond yours.

Our Challenge

Return to the Scriptures!

Part 1

Our Challenge: Return to the Scriptures!

I am constantly intrigued and challenged whenever I look at the logic and strategy of the young missionary church in the book of Acts, as I sought to "make disciples of all nations" (Matthew 28:19). Considering that the early church did not enjoy the numerical strength we have, or the technological advances we take for granted, one cannot but wonder how this small band of disciples made such a tremendous impact on their world. What was their secret? What can we learn from their strategy?

—David Zac Niringiye, Uganda, Africa

Paul's Biblical Example Introduced

See Supplement A: Maps of Paul's Missionary Journeys (pages 115–116)

It would be difficult to find any better model than the Apostle Paul in the work of establishing new churches. In just ten years, Paul established the church in four provinces: Galatia, Macedonia, Achaia and Asia. Prior to AD 47 there were no churches in these provinces, but by AD 57 Paul could speak of his work there as being done (Romans 15:19-20).

See Supplement B: Returning to the Scriptures (pages 117–124)

Compared to Paul's established churches, today's missionary endeavors are plagued by two disquieting symptoms:

1. We have not succeeded in planting Christianity so that it has become "truly indigenous." For the most part, Christianity is still considered a foreign religion in many countries outside Europe and North America.

2. The missions are not self-sustaining. They do not meet their own needs, but continue to appeal for more money and manpower. There is an unrealistic fear that without foreign support the mission will fail, the converts will fall away, and ground painfully won will be lost.

Questions for us:

Why are we not making this kind of progress today?

_____

_____

_____

Why have we not succeeded in planting indigenous Christianity like the early Jewish Church did with the Gentiles?

_____

_____

_____

Why aren't our missions self-sustaining?

_____

_____

_____

The purpose of this manual is to set forth the methods and principles Paul used that produced these amazing indigenous and self-sustaining results.

What we want to do:

1. **Restore** or establish our courage and confidence in the authority and sufficiency of Scripture and the Holy Spirit to establish churches.
(It is recommended that you complete Lesson 31 • Authority and Sufficiency of Scripture, page 90, before proceeding)

2. **Paint** a biblical vision of God's plan for His church today.

3. **Start** developing a personal strategy or tracks for our ministry to run on that are biblical, simple, practical, supra-cultural and timeless, and are not dependent on man, education, buildings or money.

See Supplement C: _Church Planting Movements (pages 125–127)_

Scripture Reveals God has a Purpose and a Plan

God's *purpose* is to show His glory!

      A. Through preaching the *"Unsearchable riches of Christ"*—Ephesians 3:8

      B. Through making known the *"Plan of the mystery"*—Ephesians 3:9

      C. Through the *"Church"*—Ephesians 3:10

God's *plan* is to build His Church!

      A. Goal: *"Build His Church"*—Matthew 16:18

      B. Promise: *"I will build My Church"*—Matthew 16:18

      See Supplement D: *People Groups (pages 128–129)*

      C. Command: *"Go and make disciples of all nations* (people groups)*"*—Matthew 28:19-20

      D. Power: *"You shall receive power"*—Acts 1:6-11

See Supplement E: *Map of the Spread of the Gospel (page 130)*

See Supplement F: *Factors that Made the Early Church Powerful (pages 131–133)*

Our Challenge

Understand God's Plan

Part 2

Our Challenge: Understand God's Plan

God's Plan for His Church Unfolds

We have learned that God has a plan for revealing His glory. God's plan and purpose is accomplished through His Church by preaching the gospel and revealing the mystery.

Now we will take a close look at the writings in Acts that focus on the establishment and growth of the New Testament church. Through these lessons, you will discern God's timeless and supra-cultural key principles of church planting which stay consistent throughout the book of Acts. It is important to recognize these so you can discover, by comparing and contrasting with today's church, where its strengths and weaknesses lie. In doing this, you will be able to see where change is needed to bring your church planting ministry more in line with the Scriptures.

As you read the book of Acts, realize that it is more than just a history book. We know that all Scripture is alive and God-breathed and useful in guiding our lives today.

See Supplement G: *Overview of the Book of Acts (page 134)*

Discussion Questions:

• Is Acts just a history book or can it be used today?

_____

_____

• Where do you draw the line in using it today?

_____

_____

• What are the problems for not using it today?

_____

_____

• What are some problems for following it closely today?

_____

_____

The historical and contemporary church should be viewed through three lenses:

(See page 123, Absolutes and Non-absolutes)

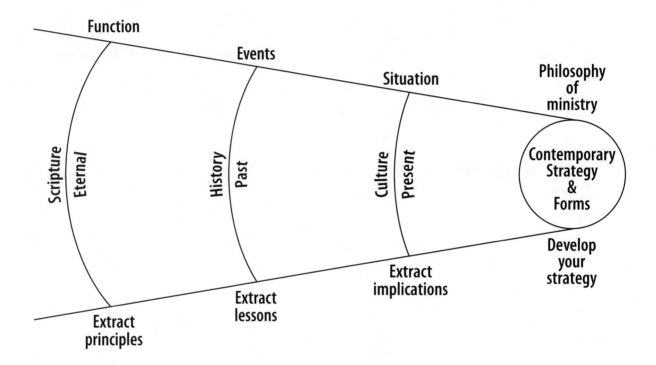

This illustration is based on work by Gene Getz as seen in *Sharpening the Focus of the Church*, ©1974, Moody Press.

God's Plan for His Church Unfolds

Lesson 1 • Expanding Churches: Jerusalem

Step 1: Observe—*What is written in the Bible?*

Read the first division in the book of Acts **(1–6:7)**. List in the chart below the keys that were useful in establishing and expanding the church in Jerusalem.

Step 2: Respond—*What are your insights?*

Contrast the keys you see in Acts with today's church using the chart below.

Step 3: Discuss—*What are our shared insights?*

How can you use the keys you see in Acts to establish and expand today's church?

Step 1: List the keys that were useful in expanding the early church	**Step 2:** Contrast these keys with today's church	**Step 3:** How can you use these keys to establish and expand today's church?

Lesson 2 • Expanding Churches: Judea and Samaria

Step 1: Observe—*What is written in the Bible?*

Read the second division in the book of Acts (**6:8–9:31**) List in the chart below the keys that were useful in establishing and expanding the church in Judea and Samaria.

Step 2: Respond—*What are your insights?*

Contrast the keys you see in Acts with today's church using the chart below.

Step 3: Discuss—*What are our shared insights?*

How can you use the keys you see in Acts to establish and expand today's church?

Step 1: List the keys that were useful in expanding the early church	**Step 2:** Contrast these keys with today's church	**Step 3:** How can you use these keys to establish and expand today's church?

Lesson 3 • Expanding Churches: Antioch

Step 1: Observe—*What is written in the Bible?*

Read the third division in the book of Acts **(9:32–12:24)** List in the chart below the keys that were useful in establishing and expanding the church in Antioch.

Step 2: Respond—*What are your insights?*

Contrast the keys you see in Acts with today's church using the chart below.

Step 3: Discuss—*What are our shared insights?*

How can you use the keys you see in Acts to establish and expand today's church?

Step 1: List the keys that were useful in expanding the early church	**Step 2:** Contrast these keys with today's church	**Step 3:** How can you use these keys to establish and expand today's church?

Lesson 4 • Expanding Churches: Asia Minor

Step 1: Observe—*What is written in the Bible?*

Read the fourth division in the book of Acts **(12:25–16:5)** List in the chart below the keys that were useful in establishing and expanding the church in Asia Minor.

Step 2: Respond—*What are your insights?*

Contrast the keys you see in Acts with today's church using the chart below.

Step 3: Discuss—*What are our shared insights?*

How can you use the keys you see in Acts to establish and expand today's church?

Step 1: List the keys that were useful in expanding the early church	**Step 2:** Contrast these keys with today's church	**Step 3:** How can you use these keys to establish and expand today's church?

Lesson 5 • Expanding Churches: Aegean Area

Step 1: Observe—*What is written in the Bible?*

Read the fifth division in the book of Acts (**16:6–19:20**) List in the chart below the keys that were useful in establishing and expanding the church in the Aegean area.

Step 2: Respond—*What are your insights?*

Contrast the keys you see in Acts with today's church using the chart below.

Step 3: Discuss—*What are our shared insights?*

How can you use the keys you see in Acts to establish and expand today's church?

Step 1: List the keys that were useful in expanding the early church	**Step 2:** Contrast these keys with today's church	**Step 3:** How can you use these keys to establish and expand today's church?

Lesson 6 • Expanding Churches: Roman Empire

Step 1: Observe—*What is written in the Bible?*

Read the sixth division in the book of Acts (**19:21–28:20**) List in the chart below the keys that were useful in establishing and expanding the church.

Step 2: Respond—*What are your insights?*

Contrast the keys you see in Acts with today's church using the chart below.

Step 3: Discuss—*What are our shared insights?*

How can you use the keys you see in Acts to establish and expand today's church?

Step 1: List the keys that were useful in expanding the early church	**Step 2:** Contrast these keys with today's church	**Step 3:** How can you use these keys to establish and expand today's church?

Additional notes:

God's Plan for His Church Unfolds

Project A · Key Principles from the Churches in Acts

Step 1: Observe—*What is written in the Bible?*

List the timeless and supra-cultural key principles that remain consistent throughout the book of Acts. (See page 123, Absolutes and Non-absolutes)

Step 2: Respond—*What are your insights?*

Contrast and compare this list of timeless and supra-cultural key principles with today's church.

Step 3: Discuss—*What are our shared insights?*

How can you use these keys to establish and expand today's church?

Step 1: List the consistent key principles from the book of Acts	Step 2: Contrast these keys with today's church	Step 3: How can you use these keys to establish and expand today's church?

Step 4: Process—*Delineate Key Concepts*

Divide your list of key principles from the previous chart into the following categories.

My Responsibility	Work of the Holy Spirit

Lesson 7 • The Great Commission

Step 1: Observe—*What is written in the Bible?*

Matthew 16:13-20; Matthew 28:16-20 (Great Commission); Acts 2:42-47; Luke 24:44-49; Acts 13:1–14:28; Acts 1:6-11; Acts 20:17-28

Step 2: Respond—*What are your insights?*

How do you think the disciples understood the Great Commission?

_____

_____

_____

What did Jesus have planned when He gave the Great Commission?

_____

_____

_____

Step 3: Discuss—*What are our shared insights?*

Is the Great Commission to an individual or a group of people?

_____

_____

Step 4: Summarize—*Write the key principles*

Based on your understanding of what the Bible teaches about the expansion of the early church, write a brief summary of how the Great Commission was unfolding in the book of Acts.

_____

_____

_____

Step 5: Action—*What changes do you need to make?*

_____

_____

_____

_____

_____

Lesson 8 • The Role of the Church

Step 1: Observe—*What is written in the Bible?*

Acts 1:6-11; Acts 2:42-47; Acts 13:1–14:28; Acts 20:17-28

Step 2: Respond—*What are your insights?*

What was the role of the church in seeing the gospel progress in Acts?

Compare the early church with the role of the church today.

Step 3: Discuss—*What are our shared insights?*

Do you agree or disagree that the church is one of the essential elements of any long-lasting mission strategy? Why or why not?

Step 1: What was the role of the church in seeing the gospel progress in Acts	**Step 2:** Compare the early church with the role of the church today

Lesson 9 • Paul's Mission Work Defined

Step 1: Observe—*What is written in the Bible?*

Acts 13:1–14:28

Step 2: Respond—*What are your insights?*

Identify the most important principles Paul used in his missionary work.

_____

_____

_____

_____

What pattern do you see developing in Paul's missionary activity?

_____

_____

_____

How does your church define missions and missionaries today?

_____

_____

_____

Compare your definition with the life and activities of Paul.

_____

_____

_____

Step 3: Discuss—*What are our shared insights?*

To what degree should the modern church follow Paul's strategy for mission work and missionaries?

_____

_____

_____

_____

_____

_____

_____

_____

Project B • Key Elements of Paul's Missionary Strategy

1. In your own words, summarize the key elements of Paul's missionary strategy.

2. How does your missionary strategy compare to Paul's?

3. What questions do you have concerning Paul's mission strategy?

4. What personal convictions are you beginning to develop?

Book of Acts Conclusion
A Definition of Church Planting

The main purpose of church planting is to plant new churches where none exist and to strengthen existing churches where they do exist.

Our Example: The Antioch Church

To form a biblical picture of an established church, examine the church at Antioch. It developed through these four stages:

1. **Building** a community base—Acts 2:42-47

2. **Overseeing** expansion of the gospel from Jews to the Gentiles—Acts 3–12

3. **Establishing** churches—Acts 11:19-30

4. **Sending** out proven leaders—Acts 13:1-3

Paul's plan had four basic stages—Acts 13:1–14:26

1. **Evangelizing**–getting the message to strategic cities—Romans 15:14-19
   Phase One: Establish a beachhead of disciples
   Phase Two: Expose the life of Christ to the community—Acts 11:26; Titus 2–3

2. **Establishing**–these communities into churches—Acts 14:23; Titus 1:5

3. **Equipping**–by teaching the new believers—Acts 14:22

4. **Expanding**–by identifying and equipping emerging leaders—Acts 16:1-5 they passed the baton to the elders—Acts 20:17-28, leaving them instructions for establishing and training faithful men—1 & 2 Timothy; Titus.

Now we can visualize four stages of church development and see how they build upon one another:

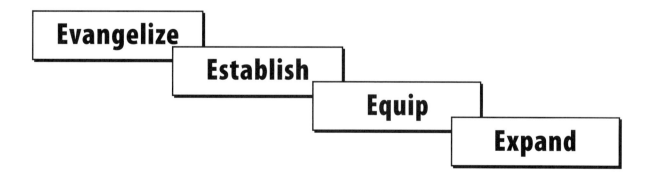

God's Plan for His Church Unfolds

Project C: Measure and Compare Your Church with the Antioch Church

Jerusalem to Antioch	Measure your Church
Christians scattered, preaching the gospel, Acts 11:19-20	Preaching:
Many turned to the Lord, Acts 11:21	Turning:
Jerusalem Church sends Barnabas to Antioch, Acts 11:22-24a	Sending:
Antioch Church adds a great number of people to the Lord, Acts 11:24b	Multiplying:
Barnabas gets Saul's help, Acts 11:25	Discipling:
Barnabas and Saul taught a great many people for a year, Acts 11:26	Teaching:
Believers were first called Christians in Antioch, Acts 11:26	Maturing:
Antioch Church sends Barnabas and Saul to the world, Acts 13:1-4	Sending and Reproducing:

Missionary Strategy	Your Strategy
They evangelized strategic cities, Acts 13:4–14:21	Evangelizing:
• Instructed the new believers, Acts 14:21-22	Instructing:
• Appointed Elders, Acts 14:23	Appointing:
They reported to Antioch, Acts 14:27-28	Accountability:
They established churches by visits and letters, Acts 15:36—28:31 and the Epistles	Establishing:
They networked with missionary teams and with churches, Acts	Teamwork:
They gave priority to a struggling church over an opened door, 2 Corinthians 2:12-13	Equipping:
The Gospel Expands	**Your Expansion**
The gospel was preached from Jerusalem to Illyricum, Romans 15:19-20	Fulfilled:
The gospel continued to expand, Acts 28:30-31	Expanding:
The next generation of leaders continued the process, 2 Timothy 2:2ff	Baton Passed:

Additional notes:

God's Pattern Revealed

After studying so much Scripture, do you see a pattern emerging?

As with many things, there is a predictable cycle that shows how a healthy church develops: **Evangelize, Establish, Equip and Expand**

Evangelize: This is the process used to get the message to the people most effectively.

Establish: This is the process that brings the new believers to a sure or firm foundation in the faith through prayerfully determining the needs of the people and how meeting those needs will look within their culture.

Equip: This is the process of teaching people how to spiritually feed themselves, appointing with empowerment local church leaders to lead their church.

Expand: The natural development of this kind of church will be to reach out farther into the community with the gospel and add to their number. This is seen over and over in Paul's writings.

This outreach will provide more people to evangelize, establish and equip. When they are taught and empowered, they too will reach out farther into the community, adding more. This growth becomes part of the cycle of natural church development. This growth can be measured by the **churches' ability to release, not retain disciples.**

These processes flow in succession like this:

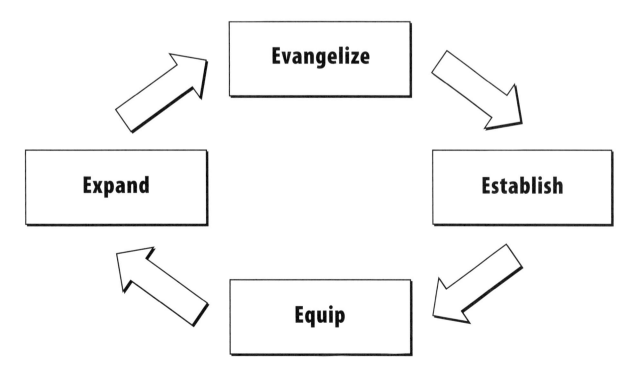

Project D: Develop Your Missions Strategy

We have learned so much from the Scriptures. Now it is time to boil it down to the key principles and discover how God will use you in your location to build His church.

1. Develop a mission strategy for a church to follow in carrying out the Great Commission at any time in any culture.

_____

_____

_____

_____

_____

_____

2. Personalize this mission strategy for your present or future situation.

_____

_____

_____

_____

_____

_____

_____

_____

3. Make a list of prayer requests concerning your role in building God's church locally and beyond.

_____

_____

_____

_____

_____

_____

_____

4. Begin praying now!

Our Challenge
Develop Strong Leaders in the Church

Part 3

Our Challenge: Develop Strong Leaders in the Church

Biblical Principles of Leadership Development

The popular Western institutional model of discipleship (or leadership development) is characterized by two sad failings:

1. Failure to emphasize the centrality of the church as revealed in Scripture

2. Failure to recognize the sufficiency and authority of Scriptures in the process of making disciples and developing leaders.

Some view the Western model of making disciples and leaders superior to what was done in the early church. Where did today's popular training methods originate? Are the methods biblical? Is the popular Western model of training producing Holy Spirit filled men of God—full of wisdom and living sacrificial lives for the sake of the gospel?

Where can one find answers today? What better place to begin than with an examination of the Scriptures directly related to church planting. Such an examination reveals that the discipleship process prompted by God's Spirit was key to planting and establishing churches. One cannot deny the early church made great progress in planting churches. The leadership development process implemented was key to this tremendous progress.

Before traveling back to the early church, let us go to the gospels where John the Baptist sets forth the key ingredient that undergirds the philosophy of leadership development expressed by the early church. John the Baptist paved the way for Jesus and set forth a solid supra-cultural and timeless principle when he said, "He (Jesus) must increase, but I must decrease" (John 3:30 NIV). The process moves from John the Baptist to Jesus, then Jesus called Andrew. Andrew called Peter, and Peter, who according to tradition, called and discipled Barnabas, Barnabas called Paul, and Paul called Timothy.

With this in mind, let us visit the early church which reaped the benefits of the disciple-making models of both Jesus and John the Baptist. Observe how the church developed an abundance of Spirit-filled, bold, godly leaders who were willing to die for their faith.

However, as the chart on the right shows, we now have a serious shortfall of leaders in the church.

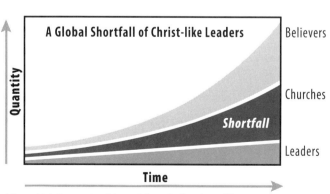

Graph adapted from MentorLink International (www.MentorLink.org), used by permission.

1. Church Planters Emerged in the Early Church (Acts 4:36-37; 9:26, 27; 11:19-26; 15:36-40)

Barnabas' character was proven (4:36-37; 9:26, 27; 15:36-40)

What can you learn from Barnabas' name? (4:36)

_____

What makes you think Barnabas was devoted to the Lord? (4:37)

_____

_____

What indicates Barnabas was a man under authority? (4:37)

_____

Why would Barnabas make a good partner in the ministry? (9:26-27; 15:36-40)

_____

_____

Barnabas was sent out by the Jerusalem Church (11:19-23)

Why was Barnabas sent to Antioch? (11:19-23a; 15:22)

_____

What did Barnabas do when he arrived at Antioch? (11:23b; 20:24)

_____

Barnabas' qualifications for church planting (11:24-26)

What kind of man was Barnabas? (11:24) Why?

_____

Barnabas was a man full of the Holy Spirit. Why is this an important qualification? (11:24)

_____

_____

Why is this qualification commonly neglected today?

_____

_____

Barnabas was a man full of faith. What does this mean? (11:24)

_____

_____

Who did Barnabas get to help him? Why? (11:25, 26)

_____

How long did they stay in Antioch? What did they do while there? (11:26)

What were their disciples first called? (11:26b) Why?

2. Church Planters Were Sent Out by the Early Church (Acts 13:1–14:27)

Church planters were developed to be sent (13:1-4)

Who were the leaders, prophets and teachers in the Antioch Church? (13:1)

Where were they trained? (13:1)

Who do you think were the two key men in this group? (13:1-2)

What were they doing when the Holy Spirit spoke to them? (13:2)

Who sent Barnabas and Paul out? (13:2-4)

Who else was involved in this sending process? (13:1-4)

Describe the sending process. (13:3)

Church planters had a strategy (14:21-27)

What was the first thing they did? (14:21a)

What was the result of preaching the gospel? (14:21b)

Why did they return to Lystra, Iconium and Antioch? (14:22)

What did they appoint in every church? (14:23)

How did they appoint them? (14:23; 20:28)

_____

Who did they commit them to? (14:23b; 20:28)

_____

Where did they return to? Why? (14:26-27)

_____

3. Church Planters Developed Elders in the Early Church (Acts 20:17-38)

Paul's discipleship strategy for elders (20:17-26)

Where did Paul live in Ephesus? (20:18)

_____

How did Paul serve them? (20:19)

_____

What did Paul preach to them? (20:20)

_____

_____

Where did Paul teach them? (20:20)

_____

What did Paul testify? (20:21)

_____

What did Paul not value? Why? (20:24)

_____

What was Paul's ministry purpose? (20:24)

_____

Paul's teaching to the elders (20:27-32)

What did Paul proclaim to them? (20:27)

_____

Who did Paul tell them to pay careful attention to? (20:28)

_____

Describe the relationship the elders had with the church of God. (20:28)

_____

Who would come into the church after Paul departed? (20:29)

_____

What would they do to the church? (20:29-30)

_____

Where would these fierce wolves come from? (20:30)

_____

What warning did Paul give these elders? (20:31)

_____

How did Paul warn them? (20:31)

_____

Who and what did Paul commend them to? (20:32)

_____

Paul's model for the elders (20:33-35)

What did Paul not covet? Why? (20:33, 34)

_____

Why did Paul work? (20:34)

_____

What did Paul show them? Why? (20:35)

_____

_____

See Supplement H: Church Planter's Support (pages 135–137)

Paul's relationship with the elders (20:36-38)

What did Paul do with the elders when he was departing? (20:36)

_____

Describe Paul's relationship with the elders. (20:37-38)

_____

4. Church Planters Developed Other Church Planters (Acts 16:1-5; 18:28; 1 Timothy; 2 Timothy; Titus)

Paul selected church planters who were tested in the church (16:2-5)

What was the name of the disciple Paul met when he came to Lystra? (16:1)

_____

Where did Timothy's faith first live? (2 Timothy 1:5)

_____

Why do you think Paul chose Timothy? (16:2)

_____

What did Paul want to do with Timothy? (16:3)

_____

How did Paul train Timothy? (16:3-4)

_____

What was the result of this process? (16:5)

_____

_____

Paul built teams of people to assist him (18:24-28; 20:4)

Who were some of Paul's helpers? (18:24-28)

_____

How were they trained in sound doctrine? (18:24-26)

_____

Describe their effectiveness in the ministry of the Word. (18:27-28)

_____

_____

Were these helpers trained _for_ the ministry or _in_ the ministry? (20:4, 18, 31)

_____

Paul's instruction to church planters (1 & 2 Timothy and Titus)

Read through these letters and list below or underline or highlight in your Bible all the words that Paul uses to describe the church planters' character as being models and examples of Christ. List some of the characteristics of the church planters.

See Supplement I: Church Planter's Ministry Described Biblically (pages 138–141)

_____

_____

List as many character traits as you can about Barnabas from Part 1 (page 46).

_____

_____

Why is character so important in the church planter's ministry? (2 Timothy 2:20-22)

_____

_____

Paul used church planters to establish existing churches (Titus)

Why did Paul leave Titus in Crete? Why? (1:5)

_____

What does it mean to set in order? (1:5-9)

_____

_____

What did Paul tell Titus to teach? (2:1)

_____

Describe what Paul meant by sound doctrine or teaching. (2:2-3)

_____

_____

5. Church Planters Trained for the Next Generation (2 Timothy)

Discipling faithful men (2 Timothy 2:2)

What types of men were to be entrusted with Paul's teaching? (2:2)

_____

What should they be enabled to do? (2:2)

_____

_____

Timothy's charge (2 Timothy 4:1-5)

What did Paul charge Timothy to do? (4:1-5)

_____

Why is this charge so important? (4:1-5)

_____

_____

Paul's farewell (2 Timothy 4:6-18)

What was Paul's perspective on his past life? His future life? (4:6-9)

_____

What happened to Paul's disciple, Demas? (4:9-10)

_____

Based on Acts 15:37-40, why would Paul now want Mark? (4:11)

_____

How did Paul handle the situation with Alexander? (4:14-15)

_____

_____

Every "Paul" (church planter) needs a

   Stephen: Why? (Acts 7:58)

   _____

   Barnabas: Why? (Acts 9:26-27; 11:25-26)

   _____

   Timothy: Why? (1 & 2 Timothy)

   _____

   Luke: Why? (2 Timothy 4:11)

   _____

   Mark: Why? (2 Timothy 4:11)

   _____

   Demas: Why? (2 Timothy 4:10)

   _____

   Alexander: Why? (2 Timothy 4:14)

   _____

   Titus: Why? (2 Timothy 4:10; Titus 1:5)

   _____

Who stood by Paul? Why? (4:16-18)

_____

Who did Paul want to receive honor and attention for his life and ministry? (4:18b)

_____

_____

Project E: Developing a Biblical Model of Leadership

1. Make an outline of the biblical model of leadership development.

2. Compare the leadership development process of your church with your outline (above). Where does your church need to change?

3. What can you do to help make that happen?

4. Write a brief strategy of your leadership role and responsibility in your church.

Our Challenge
Develop Strong Churches

Our Challenge: Develop Strong Churches

God's Plan for a Strong Church

(See page 36, Book of Acts Conclusion)

Paul was a master church builder who laid the foundations upon which others built. He was not just concerned with starting new churches; he wanted them to be strong. This is evidenced by his use of the word *strengthen* or *establish* in the following Scriptures:

By Luke: Acts 14:21-23; 15:36–16:5; 18:22-23

By Paul: Romans 1:8-15; 16:25-27; 1 Thessalonians 3:1-13 and
2 Thessalonians 2:16-17

The word *strengthen* or *establish* was translated from the word "sterizo" or "episterizo" which means to fix, to fasten or make fast. Its usage gives us a key insight into what Paul wanted new churches to become. Its use means to support or to fix something so that it stands upright by itself or becomes immovable. For example, it is used to describe a stake that supports a vine or a stick that assists an aging person. Therefore, Paul wanted the newly founded churches to be secure and stable; not easily moved or shaken.

In order to accomplish this, Paul not only visited the churches, he wrote letters to them. His letters can be divided into early letters, middle letters, and latter letters. This gives great insights into the strategy Paul used to make these newly founded churches strong. The following is a breakdown or description of his letters in chronological order. (Note: These letters will be referred to as 'tools' that are instructions to make churches strong by addressing specific, real-life issues.)

Paul's Early Letters (Tools)

Used to defend and establish in the gospel of grace

Galatians: Returning to the pure gospel, not mixing with law

1 and 2 Thessalonians: Stand firm in the gospel

1 Corinthians: Divisions solved by the implications of the gospel

2 Corinthians: Defense of the minister of the gospel

Romans: Preaching a complete treatise of the gospel

Paul's Middle Letters (Tools)

For churches to be one-minded in the person and plan of Christ

Ephesians: Grasping the mystery of the church and plan of Christ

Philippians: One-minded church participation in the progress of the gospel

Colossians: Focusing on the head of the church

Philemon: Relational implications of one-minded participation in the progress of the gospel

Paul's Latter Letters (Tools)

For churches to be properly ordered households of God

1 Timothy: Properly ordering the community life of the household of God, the church of Jesus Christ

Titus: Setting in order what remains—fully establishing the churches by teaching sound doctrine

2 Timothy: The significance and function of well-trained, faithful leaders

***See Supplement J:** Timeline of Paul's Ministry and Letters (page 142)*

Lesson 10 • Establishing Churches: Paul's Letters

Step 1: Observe—*What is written in the Bible?*

Acts 14:21-27; 15:32, 33, 41; 18:23; Romans 1:11; 16:25; 1 Thessalonians 3:2, 13; 2 Thessalonians 2:16-17; 3:3

Step 2: Respond—*What are your insights?*

What were some of Paul's core elements in establishing churches?

_____

_____

_____

Step 3: Discuss—*What are our shared insights?*

When do you think Paul would have considered a church established?

_____

_____

Do you think Paul's letters to the churches serve as the standard for establishing churches? Why? Or why not?

_____

_____

_____

Step 4: Summarize—*Write the core elements*

Based on your understanding of Paul's letters on making strong churches, write a brief summary of the core elements every church can follow at any time and in any culture.

_____

_____

_____

_____

Step 5: Action—*What changes do you need to make?*

_____

_____

_____

_____

_____

Lesson 11 • Establishing Churches: Paul's Early Letters

Step 1: Observe—*What is written in the Bible?*

Read Paul's "early" letters in the chronological order they were written.

a) Galatians

b) 1 & 2 Thessalonians

c) 1 & 2 Corinthians

d) Romans

Step 2: Discuss—*What are our shared insights?*

What insights do Paul's letters give us into the process of establishing churches, especially in relation to the order in which the letters were written?

_____

_____

_____

Step 3: Respond—*Answer the following questions.*

	Galatians	**1, 2 Thessalonians**	**1, 2 Corinthians**	**Romans**
What was Paul's main purpose in writing these letters?				
How did Paul use these tools (letters) to establish churches?				
What key principles can we use today to establish churches?				

Lesson 12 • Establishing Churches: Paul's Middle Letters

Step 1: Observe—*What is written in the Bible?*

Read Paul's "middle" letters in the chronological order they were written.

a) Ephesians

b) Philippians

c) Colossians

d) Philemon

Step 2: Discuss—*What are our shared insights?*

What insights do Paul's letters give us into the process of establishing churches, especially in relation to the order in which the letters were written?

_____

_____

_____

Step 3: Respond—*Answer the following questions.*

	Ephesians	**Philippians**	**Colossians**	**Philemon**
What was Paul's main purpose in writing these letters?				
How did Paul use these tools (letters) to establish churches?				
What key principles can we use today to establish churches?				

God's Plan for a Strong Church

Lesson 13 • Establishing Churches: Paul's Latter Letters

Step 1: Observe—*What is written in the Bible?*

Read Paul's "latter" letters, which he wrote to key men, in the chronological order they were written.

a) 1 Timothy

b) Titus

c) 2 Timothy

Step 2: Discuss—*What are our shared insights?*

What insights do Paul's letters give us into the process of establishing churches, especially in relation to the order in which the letters were written?

_____

_____

_____

Step 3: Respond—*Answer the following questions.*

	1 Timothy	Titus	2 Timothy
What was Paul's main purpose in writing these letters?			
How did Paul use these tools (letters) to establish churches?			
What key principles can we use today to establish churches?			

Project F • How to Fully Establish a Church

1. Write a one-paragraph summary of Paul's concept of the "establishing" process.

_____

_____

_____

_____

_____

2. Summarize how each of Paul's groups of letters (Early, Middle, and Latter) contributed to the establishing process.

   Early Letters:

   _____

   _____

   Middle Letters:

   _____

   _____

   Latter Letters:

   _____

   _____

3. Begin to develop in writing, a strategy for fully establishing a church. This is a living project which will be modified as the course is completed.

   _____

   _____

   _____

   _____

   _____

   _____

See Supplement K: *Effects of Not Being Established (pages 143–145)*

Lesson 14 • When is a Church an Established Church?

Step 1: Observe–*What is written in the Bible?*

Acts 2:42-47: 13:1-16:5; 20:17-38; 1 & 2 Timothy; Titus

Step 2: Respond–*What are your insights?*

Describe the essential elements which must exist before a group of people can be called an established church, at any time, in any culture.

_____

_____

_____

_____

_____

Step 3: Discuss–*What are our shared insights?*

Which of the following groups would you consider an established church?

a) A group of people meeting for Bible study or prayer? Why or why not?

_____

_____

b) A group of believers joining together with other believers to accomplish a particular ministry project? Why or why not?

_____

_____

c) A group of new believers who gather together for Bible study and prayer where the gospel has just penetrated? Why or why not?

_____

_____

d) A group of new believers gathering together for Bible study where several established churches already exist? Why or why not?

_____

_____

e) A family meeting together for family devotions? Why or why not?

_____

_____

Project G • Establishing a New Testament Church

1. Describe a New Testament established church. Begin your project with, "A New Testament established church is…" Be certain the basic core elements are true for all churches at any time, in any culture.

_____

_____

_____

_____

_____

2. Compare your church with your outline (above). Where does your church need to change?

_____

_____

_____

_____

_____

3. What can you do to help make that happen?

_____

_____

_____

_____

_____

4. Write a brief strategy of your role and responsibility in helping your church conform to the biblical model in starting a new church.

_____

_____

_____

_____

_____

_____

_____

_____

Our Challenge

Develop Ordered Churches

Part 5

Our Challenge: Develop Ordered Churches

Paul's Twofold Ministry

The Apostle Paul states in Ephesians 3:1-12 that his ministry is basically twofold:

1. To preach to the Gentiles—Ephesians 3:8

2. To bring to light the administration of the mystery (that Jews and Gentiles are one in Christ)—Ephesians 3:9

The word translated as administration, plan, or stewardship comes from the Greek word "oikonomia" which comes from two words:

"oikos" which means house, household, family, or home

"nomos" which means law or order

So "oikonomia" means house law or house order.

Therefore, in addition to preaching the gospel of grace, Paul's job included revealing God's order for his family or household, which now consisted of both Jews and Gentiles. Paul clearly understood his job to be one of declaring how God wanted His Church structured and how it was to function. This theme runs continuously and consistently throughout Paul's letters.

When Paul writes to Timothy and Titus, he is instructing the believers how to properly live within the household or family of God, the church. This concept of family is a universal concept since everyone knows about a family. It is important to understand that the church is a family made up of individual families. In other words, God's household is made up of many individual households (1 Timothy 3:14-15).

Order in the church flows from order in the family. Proper order in the family will provide good order in the church. Disorder in the family will affect the order in the church. Therefore peace, harmony, and unity in the family will be enhanced when everyone fulfills his or her biblical roles.

Paul expected believers to follow the principles he established for churches. He presented these principles in the thirteen letters he wrote to the various churches and individuals (1 Timothy 3:14-15). These churches, which had not yet fully followed his instruction, were considered as needing to be set in order (Titus1:5).

Paul's latter letters to Timothy and Titus were written to give us these household management instructions. Ministry in the church should be complementary and not conflicting. Women complement men, deacons complement elders, and elders, Christ. No one should be at odds with anyone in ministry. If a man can't manage his home, he might not be qualified to manage the church (1 Timothy 3:4-5 and Titus 1:6). Strong biblical leadership in the church comes from strong biblical leadership in the home.

This diagram shows the relationships between a husband, wife, and God. Both the husband and wife have an individual relationship with God as well as a close relationship with each other. Notice that as the husband and wife grow closer to God, they actually draw closer to each other. This means that a vital part of a husband and wife's relationship is their individual relationship with God.

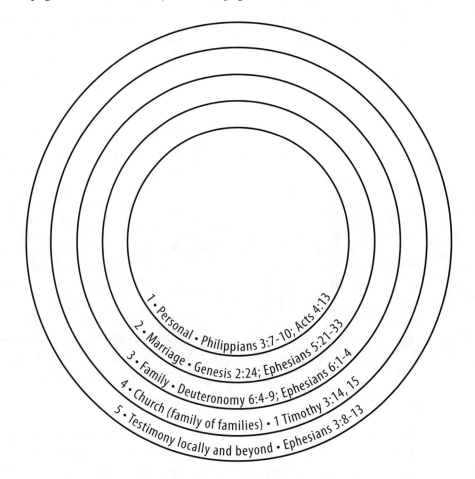

Looking at relationships in the home helps us see our roles and responsibilities in the church. Since the church is a family and not a business, knowing our role and responsibilities can enhance our church structure. See what Paul has to say about the individual family and the family in the larger household of God.

God's Plan for an Ordered Church

Below is a visual diagram of the progression of an ordered church found in Lessons 15-42 (pages 71–101) and Projects H–J (pages 79, 89, and 102).

1 • Personal • Philippians 3:7-10; Acts 4:13
2 • Marriage • Genesis 2:24; Ephesians 5:21-33
3 • Family • Deuteronomy 6:4-9; Ephesians 6:1-4
4 • Church (family of families) • 1 Timothy 3:14, 15
5 • Testimony locally and beyond • Ephesians 3:8-13

Lesson 15 • Family of Families

Step 1: Observe—*What is written in the Bible?*

1 Timothy 3:14-15; Titus 1:5-6

Step 2: Respond—*What are your insights?*

What are the key social relationships within the home and the primary responsibilities of each?

_____

_____

What are the key social relationships within the church and the responsibilities of each?

_____

_____

Step 3: Discuss—*What are our shared insights?*

What implications for managing the church arise from viewing the home as a household within a larger household, the church?

_____

_____

Step 4: Summarize—*Write the key principles.*

How might these concepts affect our understanding of:

Church Authority

_____

_____

Church Discipline

_____

_____

Church Shepherding

_____

_____

Step 5: Action—*What changes do you need to make?*

_____

_____

_____

_____

Lesson 16 • Household Order

Step 1: Observe—*What is written in the Bible?*

Ephesians 5:22–6:9; Colossians 3:18–4:1; 1 & 2 Timothy; Titus

Step 2: Respond—*What are your insights?*

What was Paul's twofold job description according to Ephesians 3:8-9?

_____

_____

In what sense was Paul fulfilling his job description when he wrote to Timothy
(1 Timothy 1:2; 3:14-16) and Titus (Titus 1:4, 5)?

_____

_____

Step 3: Discuss—*What are our shared insights?*

Did Paul intend his "household order" instructions to Timothy and Titus to be followed by
all churches? Why or why not?

_____

_____

What problems might arise if these "household order" instructions are replaced with the
world's business trends and organizational guidelines?

_____

_____

_____

Step 4: Summarize—*Write the key principles.*

Based on your understanding of what the Bible teaches about "household order," write a brief
summary of the implications of how we organize and manage the household of God today?

_____

_____

_____

Step 5: Action—*What changes do you need to make?*

_____

_____

_____

_____

Biblical Roles in the Church Families

Lesson 17 • Personal

Step 1: Observe—*What is written in the Bible?*

Acts 4:13, 20:28; Luke 10:38-42; Mark 1:35; Philippians 3:7-10; Matthew 6:33; John 15:1-8; Romans 12:1-2

Step 2: Respond—*What are your insights?*

What is the primary responsibility of each member in the family?

_____

_____

_____

How does this responsibility enhance or contribute to the concept of the church being structured as a "family of families?"

_____

_____

Step 3: Discuss—*What are our shared insights?*

Is the family following or ignoring these responsibilities?

_____

What problems might arise in the church if the responsibilities of individual family members are replaced with the world's trends and thoughts?

_____

_____

_____

Step 4: Summarize—*Write the key principles.*

Based on your understanding of the biblical role of the family members, write a brief summary of the key responsibilities that every family could follow at any time, in any culture.

_____

_____

_____

Step 5: Action—*What changes do you need to make?*

_____

_____

_____

_____

Biblical Roles in the Church Families

Lesson 18 • Marriage

Step 1: Observe—*What is written in the Bible?*

Genesis 2:18-25; Matthew 19:3-6; 1 Corinthians 7:1-16; Ephesians 5:29-33;
1 Corinthians 13:4-13

Step 2: Respond—*What are your insights?*

What is the primary responsibility of the marriage in the family?

_____

_____

_____

How does this responsibility enhance or contribute to the concept of the church being
structured as a "family of families?"

_____

_____

Step 3: Discuss—*What are our shared insights?*

Is the family following or ignoring these responsibilities?

_____

What problems might arise in the church if these family responsibilities of the marriage are
replaced with the world's trends and thoughts?

_____

_____

_____

Step 4: Summarize—*Write the key principles.*

Based on your understanding of the biblical role of marriage, write a brief summary of
the key responsibilities that every family could follow at any time, in any culture.

_____

_____

_____

Step 5: Action—*What changes do you need to make?*

_____

_____

_____

_____

Biblical Roles in the Church Families

Lesson 19 • Husbands

Step 1: Observe—*What is written in the Bible?*

Ephesians 5:21, 25-33; Colossians 3:19; 1 Peter 3:7; 1 Corinthians 11:3

Step 2: Respond—*What are your insights?*

What is the primary responsibility of the husband in the family?

_____

_____

_____

How does this responsibility enhance or contribute to the concept of the church being structured as a "family of families?"

_____

_____

Step 3: Discuss—*What are our shared insights?*

Is the family following or ignoring these responsibilities?

_____

What problems might arise in the church if these family responsibilities of the husband are replaced with the world's trends and thoughts?

_____

_____

_____

Step 4: Summarize—*Write the key principles.*

Based on your understanding of the biblical role of the husband, write a brief summary of his key responsibilities that every family could follow at any time, in any culture.

_____

_____

_____

Step 5: Action—*What changes do you need to make?*

_____

_____

_____

_____

Biblical Roles in the Church Families

Lesson 20 • Wives

Step 1: Observe—*What is written in the Bible?*

Ephesians 5:21-24; Colossians 3:18; 1 Peter 3:1-6; Proverbs 31:10-31

Step 2: Respond—*What are your insights?*

What is the primary responsibility of the wife in the family?

_____

_____

_____

How does this responsibility enhance or contribute to the concept of the church being structured as a "family of families?"

_____

_____

Step 3: Discuss—*What are our shared insights?*

Is the family following or ignoring these responsibilities?

_____

What problems might arise in the church if these family responsibilities of the wife are replaced with the world's trends and thoughts?

_____

_____

_____

Step 4: Summarize—*Write the key principles.*

Based on your understanding of the biblical role of the wife, write a brief summary of her key responsibilities that every family could follow at any time, in any culture.

_____

_____

_____

Step 5: Action—*What changes do you need to make?*

_____

_____

_____

_____

Biblical Roles in the Church Families

Lesson 21 • Parents

Step 1: Observe—*What is written in the Bible?*

Ephesians 6:4; Colossians 3:21; Deuteronomy 6:4-9; Proverbs 22:6; 13:24

Step 2: Respond—*What are your insights?*

What is the primary responsibility of the parents in the family?

_____

_____

_____

How does this responsibility enhance or contribute to the concept of the church being structured as a "family of families?"

_____

_____

_____

Step 3: Discuss—*What are our shared insights?*

Is the family following or ignoring these responsibilities?

_____

What problems might arise in the church if these family responsibilities of parents are replaced with the world's trends and thoughts?

_____

_____

_____

Step 4: Summarize—*Write the key principles.*

Based on your understanding of the biblical role of parents, write a brief summary of their key responsibilities that every family could follow at any time, in any culture.

_____

_____

_____

Step 5: Action—*What changes do you need to make?*

_____

_____

_____

_____

Biblical Roles in the Church Families
Lesson 22 • Children

Step 1: Observe—*What is written in the Bible?*

Ephesians 6:1-3; Colossians 3:20; 1 Timothy 5:4; Psalm 144:12; Proverbs 1:7-10

Step 2: Respond—*What are your insights?*

What is the primary responsibility of the children in the family?

_____

_____

_____

How does this responsibility enhance or contribute to the concept of the church being structured as a "family of families?"

_____

_____

Step 3: Discuss—*What are our shared insights?*

Is the family following or ignoring these responsibilities?

_____

What problems might arise in the church if these family responsibilities of children are replaced with the world's trends and thoughts?

_____

_____

_____

Step 4: Summarize—*Write the key principles.*

Based on your understanding of the biblical role of children, write a brief summary of their key responsibilities that every family could follow at any time, in any culture.

_____

_____

_____

Step 5: Action—*What changes do you need to make?*

_____

_____

_____

_____

Biblical Roles in the Church Families

Project H • Setting the Church Families in Order

1. Make an outline or diagram of Paul's concept of managing the family using the different roles and their responsibilities within the family.

_____

_____

_____

_____

_____

_____

2. Compare your church with your outline or diagram (above). Where does your church need to change?

_____

_____

_____

_____

_____

3. What can you do to help make that happen?

_____

_____

_____

_____

4. Write a brief strategy of your role and responsibility in your family

_____

_____

_____

_____

_____

_____

Additional notes:

Biblical Roles in the Church Family

Lesson 23 • Ministers of the Gospel

Step 1: Observe–*What is written in the Bible?*

1 Timothy 1:5-18; 2:1-7; 3:14-15; 4:12; 2 Timothy 2:15-26; 4:2-7; Ephesians 3:7; 4:11-14

Step 2: Respond–*What are your insights?*

What is the primary responsibility of ministers of the gospel in the church (family of families)?

_____

_____

How does this responsibility enhance the church being structured as a "family of families?"

_____

_____

_____

Step 3: Discuss–*What are our shared insights?*

Is the church following or ignoring these responsibilities?

_____

What problems might arise if these responsibilities within the church are replaced with the world's trends and thoughts on ministers of gospel?

_____

_____

_____

Step 4: Summarize–*Write the key principles.*

Based on your understanding of the biblical role of ministers of the gospel, write a brief summary of their key responsibilities that every church could follow at any time, in any culture.

_____

_____

_____

_____

Step 5: Action–*What changes do you need to make?*

_____

_____

_____

_____

See Supplement I: *Church Planter's Ministry Described Biblically (pages 138–141)*

Biblical Roles in the Church Family

Lesson 24 • Pastors/Elders/Bishops

Step 1: Observe—*What is written in the Bible?*

Acts 20:17-38; 1 Timothy 3:1-7; 5:17-20; Titus 1:5-9; 1 Peter 5:1-4; Ephesians 4:11-14

Step 2: Respond—*What are your insights?*

What is the primary responsibility of pastors and elders in the church (Family of Families)?

_____

_____

How does this responsibility enhance the church being structured as a "family of families?"

_____

_____

_____

Step 3: Discuss—*What are our shared insights?*

Is the church following or ignoring these responsibilities?

_____

What problems might arise if these responsibilities within the church are replaced with the world's trends and thoughts on pastors and elders?

_____

_____

_____

Step 4: Summarize—*Write the key principles.*

Based on your understanding of the biblical role of pastors and elders, write a brief summary of their key responsibilities that every church could follow at any time, in any culture.

_____

_____

_____

_____

Step 5: Action—*What changes do you need to make?*

_____

_____

_____

_____

See Supplement L: *Qualifications of Elders (pages 146–148)*

Biblical Roles in the Church Family
Lesson 25 • Deacons

Step 1: Observe—*What is written in the Bible?*

1 Timothy 3:8-13; Acts 6:1-7

Step 2: Respond—*What are your insights?*

What is the primary responsibility of deacons in the church (Family of Families)?

_____

_____

How does this responsibility enhance the church being structured as a "family of families?"

_____

_____

_____

Step 3: Discuss—*What are our shared insights?*

Is the church following or ignoring these responsibilities?

_____

What problems might arise if these responsibilities within the church are replaced with the world's trends and thoughts on deacons?

_____

_____

_____

Step 4: Summarize—*Write the key principles.*

Based on your understanding of the biblical role of deacons, write a brief summary of their key responsibilities that every church could follow at any time, in any culture.

_____

_____

_____

_____

Step 5: Action—*What changes do you need to make?*

_____

_____

_____

_____

See Supplement M: *Qualifications of Deacons (page 149)*

Lesson 26 • Older Men

Step 1: Observe—*What is written in the Bible?*

1 Timothy 5:1; Titus 2:2; 3:8-13

Step 2: Respond—*What are your insights?*

What is the primary responsibility of older men in the church (Family of Families)?

_____

_____

How does this responsibility enhance the church being structured as a "family of families?"

_____

_____

_____

Step 3: Discuss—*What are our shared insights?*

Is the church following or ignoring these responsibilities?

_____

What problems might arise if these responsibilities within the church are replaced with the world's trends and thoughts on older men?

_____

_____

_____

Step 4: Summarize—*Write the key principles.*

Based on your understanding of the biblical role of older men, write a brief summary of their key responsibilities that every church could follow at any time, in any culture.

_____

_____

_____

_____

Step 5: Action—*What changes do you need to make?*

_____

_____

_____

_____

Biblical Roles in the Church Family

Lesson 27 • Older Women

Step 1: Observe—*What is written in the Bible?*

1 Timothy 5:2; Titus 2:3-5

Step 2: Respond—*What are your insights?*

What is the primary responsibility of older women in the church (Family of Families)?

_____

_____

How does this responsibility enhance the church being structured as a "family of families?"

_____

_____

_____

Step 3: Discuss—*What are our shared insights?*

Is the church following or ignoring these responsibilities?

_____

What problems might arise if these responsibilities within the church are replaced with the world's trends and thoughts on older women?

_____

_____

_____

Step 4: Summarize—*Write the key principles.*

Based on your understanding of the biblical role of older women, write a brief summary of their key responsibilities that every church could follow at any time, in any culture.

_____

_____

_____

_____

Step 5: Action—*What changes do you need to make?*

_____

_____

_____

_____

Biblical Roles in the Church Family

Lesson 28 • Younger Men

Step 1: Observe–*What is written in the Bible?*

1 Timothy 5:1; Titus 2:3-5; Psalm 119:9ff

Step 2: Respond–*What are your insights?*

What is the primary responsibility of younger men in the church (Family of Families)?

_____

_____

How does this responsibility enhance the church being structured as a "family of families?"

_____

_____

_____

Step 3: Discuss–*What are our shared insights?*

Is the church following or ignoring these responsibilities?

_____

What problems might arise if these responsibilities within the church are replaced with the world's trends and thoughts on younger men?

_____

_____

_____

Step 4: Summarize–*Write the key principles.*

Based on your understanding of the biblical role of younger men, write a brief summary of their key responsibilities that every church could follow at any time, in any culture.

_____

_____

_____

_____

Step 5: Action–*What changes do you need to make?*

_____

_____

_____

_____

Biblical Roles in the Church Family
Lesson 29 • Younger Women

Step 1: Observe–*What is written in the Bible?*

1 Timothy 5:2; Titus 2:4-5; Psalm 119:9ff

Step 2: Respond–*What are your insights?*

What is the primary responsibility of younger women in the church (Family of Families)?

_____

_____

How does this responsibility enhance the church being structured as a "family of families?"

_____

_____

_____

Step 3: Discuss–*What are our shared insights?*

Is the church following or ignoring these responsibilities?

_____

What problems might arise if these responsibilities within the church are replaced with the world's trends and thoughts on younger women?

_____

_____

_____

Step 4: Summarize–*Write the key principles.*

Based on your understanding of the biblical role of younger women, write a brief summary of their key responsibilities that every church could follow at any time, in any culture.

_____

_____

_____

_____

Step 5: Action–*What changes do you need to make?*

_____

_____

_____

_____

Biblical Roles in the Church Family

Lesson 30 • Widows

Step 1: Observe—*What is written in the Bible?*

> 1 Timothy 5:1-16; 1 Corinthians 7:39-40

Step 2: Respond—*What are your insights?*

> What is the primary responsibility of widows in the church (Family of Families)?

> _____

> _____

> How does this responsibility enhance the church being structured as a "family of families?"

> _____

> _____

> _____

Step 3: Discuss—*What are our shared insights?*

> Is the church following or ignoring these responsibilities?

> _____

> What problems might arise if these responsibilities within the church are replaced with the world's trends and thoughts on widows?

> _____

> _____

> _____

Step 4: Summarize—*Write the key principles.*

> Based on your understanding of the biblical role of widows, write a brief summary of their key responsibilities that every church could follow at any time, in any culture.

> _____

> _____

> _____

> _____

Step 5: Action—*What changes do you need to make?*

> _____

> _____

> _____

> _____

Biblical Roles in the Church Family

Project I • Setting the Church Family in Order

1. Make an outline or diagram of Paul's concept of managing the church using the different roles and responsibilities within the family of families.

_____

_____

_____

_____

_____

_____

_____

2. Compare your church with your outline or diagram (above). Where does your church need to change?

_____

_____

_____

_____

_____

_____

_____

3. What can you do to help make that happen?

_____

_____

_____

_____

_____

_____

_____

4. Write a brief strategy of your role and responsibility in your family.

_____

_____

_____

_____

_____

_____

_____

Biblical Issues in the Church Family

Lesson 31 • Authority and Sufficiency of Scripture

Step 1: Observe—*What is written in the Bible?*

Acts 6:7; 12:24; 13:49; 19:20; Hebrews 4:12; Jeremiah 23:29; 2 Timothy 3:16-17; 1 Peter 1:22-25; 2 Peter 1:3-4, 19-21; 1 Thessalonians 2:13; Psalm 19:7-13; Psalm 119

Step 2: Respond—*What are your insights?*

What common set of guidelines for the Bible can every church follow?

_____

_____

How do these guidelines for the Bible enhance the concept of the church being structured as a family?

_____

_____

Step 3: Discuss—*What are our shared insights?*

Is the church following or ignoring these responsibilities?

_____

What problems might arise if these biblical guidelines are replaced with the world's business and organizational thoughts on the authority and sufficiency of Scripture?

_____

_____

_____

Step 4: Summarize—*Write the key principles.*

Based on your understanding of the biblical role of Scripture, write a brief summary of key principles about the Bible that every church could follow at any time, in any culture.

_____

_____

_____

_____

Step 5: Action—*What changes do you need to make?*

_____

_____

_____

_____

Lesson 32 • Servant Leaders

Step 1: Observe—*What is written in the Bible?*

John 13:14,15; Matthew 11:29; 23:1-12; Mark 9:33-35; 10:35-45; Luke 22:24-27; 1 Corinthians 1:26-31; Philippians 2:3-11; 1 Thessalonians 2:2-12

Step 2: Respond—*What are your insights?*

What common set of guidelines for leaders can every church follow?

_____

_____

How do these guidelines for leaders enhance the concept of the church being structured as a family?

_____

_____

Step 3: Discuss—*What are our shared insights?*

Is the church following or ignoring these responsibilities?

_____

What problems might arise if these family guidelines are replaced with the world's business and organizational thoughts on leadership?

_____

_____

_____

Step 4: Summarize—*Write the key principles.*

Based on your understanding of the biblical role of leadership, write a brief summary of key principles about leaders that every church could follow at any time, in any culture.

_____

_____

_____

_____

Step 5: Action—*What changes do you need to make?*

_____

_____

_____

_____

Biblical Issues in the Church Family

Lesson 33 • Men and Women

Step 1: Observe—*What is written in the Bible?*

Acts 1:14; 2:17; 21:9; Luke 2:36-38; 1 Corinthians 11:1-16; 14:34-36; Ephesians 5:21–6:4; 1 Timothy 2:8-14; 3:4-5; 5:9-10, 14-15; Colossians 3:18–4:1; Titus 2:3-5

Step 2: Respond—*What are your insights?*

What common set of guidelines for men and women can every church follow?

_____

_____

How do these guidelines for men and women enhance the concept of the church being structured as a family?

_____

_____

Step 3: Discuss—*What are our shared insights?*

Is the church following or ignoring these guidelines?

_____

What problems might arise if these family guidelines are replaced with the world's trends and thoughts on men and women?

_____

_____

_____

Step 4: Summarize—*Write the key principles.*

Based on your understanding of the biblical roles of men and women, write a brief summary of key principles and responsibilities of men and women that every church could follow at any time, in any culture.

_____

_____

_____

Step 5: Action—*What changes do you need to make?*

_____

_____

_____

_____

Biblical Issues in the Church Family

Lesson 34 • Serving One Another

Step 1: Observe—*What is written in the Bible?*

Romans 12:5, 10; 15:5, 7, 14; 16:3-6; Galatians 5:13; 6:2; Ephesians 4:2; 5:21;
1 Thessalonians 5:11

Step 2: Respond—*What are your insights?*

What common set of guidelines for serving one another can every church follow?

_____

_____

How do these guidelines for serving one another enhance the concept of the church being
structured as a family?

_____

_____

Step 3: Discuss—*What are our shared insights?*

Is the church following or ignoring these guidelines?

_____

What problems might arise if these family guidelines for one-another service are replaced
with the world's business trends and thoughts?

_____

_____

_____

Step 4: Summarize—*Write the key principles.*

Based on your understanding of what the Bible teaches concerning serving one another,
write a brief summary of the key principles that every church could follow at any time, in
any culture.

_____

_____

_____

Step 5: Action—*What changes do you need to make?*

_____

_____

_____

_____

Lesson 35 • Spiritual Gifts

Step 1: Observe—*What is written in the Bible?*

1 Corinthians 12–14; Romans 12:1-8; Ephesians 4:1-16; 1 Peter 4:7-11

Step 2: Respond—*What are your insights?*

What common set of guidelines for spiritual gifts can every church follow?

_____

_____

How do these guidelines for spiritual gifts enhance the concept of the church being structured as a family?

_____

_____

_____

Step 3: Discuss—*What are our shared insights?*

Is the church following or ignoring these guidelines?

_____

What problems might arise if these family guidelines for spiritual gifts are replaced with the world's business trends and thoughts?

_____

_____

_____

Step 4: Summarize—*Write the key principles.*

Based on your understanding of what the Bible teaches concerning spiritual gifts, write a brief summary of the key principles that every church could follow at any time, in any culture.

_____

_____

_____

Step 5: Action—*What changes do you need to make?*

_____

_____

_____

_____

See Supplement N: *Spiritual Gifts Evaluation (pages 150–151)*

Biblical Issues in the Church Family

Lesson 36 • Strong and the Weak

Step 1: Observe—*What is written in the Bible?*

Romans 14:1–15:7; 1 Corinthians 10:23-33

Step 2: Respond—*What are your insights?*

What common set of guidelines of the strong and weak can every church follow?

_____

_____

How do these guidelines for the strong and weak enhance the concept of the church being structured as a family?

_____

_____

Step 3: Discuss—*What are our shared insights?*

Is the church following or ignoring these guidelines?

_____

What problems might arise if these family guidelines for the strong and weak are replaced with the world's business trends and thoughts?

_____

_____

_____

Step 4: Summarize—*Write the key principles.*

Based on your understanding of what the Bible teaches concerning the strong and weak, write a brief summary of the key principles that every church could follow at any time, in any culture.

_____

_____

_____

_____

Step 5: Action—*What changes do you need to make?*

_____

_____

_____

_____

Lesson 37 · Questionable Things

Step 1: Observe—*What is written in the Bible?*

1 Corinthians 6:12-20; 10:23-33; Romans 14:1–15:7 (1 Peter 2:16-21)

Step 2: Respond—*What are your insights?*

What common set of guidelines for questionable things can every church follow?

_____

_____

How do these guidelines for questionable things enhance the concept of the church being structured as a family?

_____

_____

Step 3: Discuss—*What are our shared insights?*

Is the church following or ignoring these guidelines?

_____

What problems might arise if these family guidelines for questionable things are replaced with the world's business trends and thoughts?

_____

_____

_____

Step 4: Summarize—*Write the key principles.*

Based on your understanding of what the Bible teaches concerning questionable things, write a brief summary of the key principles that every church could follow at any time, in any culture.

_____

_____

_____

_____

Step 5: Action—*What changes do you need to make?*

_____

_____

_____

_____

Lesson 38 • Handling Conflict

Step 1: Observe—*What is written in the Bible?*

Matthew 18:15-18; Acts 15:1-41; Philippians 4:2-7; Romans 14:1–15:7 (questionable things); 2 Thessalonians 3:5-16; 1 Corinthians 5:1–6:11; 1 Timothy 5:19-22; 2 Corinthians 2:1-14; 7:5-13, 2 Timothy 2:14-16; Galatians 2:1-14; 5:12–6:5; Titus 1:9-16; 3:9-11

Step 2: Respond—*What are your insights?*

What common set of guidelines for handling conflict can every church follow?

_____

_____

How do these guidelines for handling conflict enhance the concept of the church being structured as a family?

_____

_____

Step 3: Discuss—*What are our shared insights?*

Is the church following or ignoring these guidelines?

_____

What problems might arise if these family guidelines for handling conflict are replaced with the world's trends and thoughts?

_____

_____

_____

Step 4: Summarize—*Write the key principles.*

Based on your understanding of what the Bible teaches concerning handling conflict in the church, write a brief summary of the key principles that every church could follow at any time, in any culture.

_____

_____

_____

Step 5: Action—*What changes do you need to make?*

_____

_____

_____

See Supplement O: *Church Restoration and Discipline (pages 152–153)*

Biblical Issues in the Church Family

Lesson 39 • Assembly Meetings

Step 1: Observe–*What is written in the Bible?*

Acts 11:19-26; 19:8-10; 20:7-12; Romans 16:5; Ephesians 5:15-21;
1 Corinthians 11:17–14:38; 1 Timothy 2:1-15; 4:6-16; Colossians 1:18

Step 2: Respond–*What are your insights?*

What common set of guidelines for assembly meetings can every church follow?

_____

_____

How do these guidelines for assembly meetings enhance the concept of the church being structured as a family?

_____

_____

Step 3: Discuss–*What are our shared insights?*

Is the church following or ignoring these guidelines?

_____

What problems might arise if these family guidelines for assembly meetings are replaced with the world's business trends and thoughts?

_____

_____

_____

Step 4: Summarize–*Write the key principles.*

Based on your understanding of what the Bible teaches concerning assembly meetings, write a brief summary of the key principles that every church could follow at any time, in any culture.

_____

_____

_____

_____

Step 5: Action–*What changes do you need to make?*

_____

_____

_____

Biblical Issues in the Church Family

Lesson 40 • Giving and Financial Matters

Step 1: Observe—*What is written in the Bible?*

Acts 6:1-7; 11:27-30; Galatians 6:6-10; 1 Corinthians 16:1-4; 2 Thessalonians 3:6-15; 2 Corinthians 8:1–9:15; 1 Timothy 3:3, 5; 5:1-18

Step 2: Respond—*What are your insights?*

What common set of guidelines for giving and financial matters can every church follow?

_____

_____

How do these guidelines for giving and financial matters enhance the concept of the church being structured as a family?

_____

_____

Step 3: Discuss—*What are our shared insights?*

Is the church following or ignoring these guidelines?

_____

What problems might arise if these family guidelines for giving and financial matters are replaced with the world's business trends and thoughts?

_____

_____

_____

Step 4: Summarize—*Write the key principles.*

Based on your understanding of what the Bible teaches concerning giving and financial matters, write a brief summary of the key principles that every church could follow at any time, in any culture.

_____

_____

_____

Step 5: Action—*What changes do you need to make?*

_____

_____

_____

_____

Lesson 41 • Community Life and Ministry

Step 1: Observe—*What is written in the Bible?*

Romans 12:3-21; 1 Corinthians 12:1–13:13; Ephesians 4:1-16; Philippians 2:1-8

Step 2: Respond—*What are your insights?*

What common set of guidelines for community life and ministry can every church follow?

_____

_____

How do these guidelines for community life and ministry enhance the concept of the church being structured as a family?

_____

_____

_____

Step 3: Discuss—*What are our shared insights?*

Is the church following or ignoring these guidelines?

_____

What problems might arise if these family guidelines for community life and ministry are replaced with organizational and business guidelines?

_____

_____

_____

Step 4: Summarize—*Write the key principles.*

Based on your understanding of what the Bible teaches about community life and ministry, write a brief summary of the key principles that every church could follow at any time, in any culture.

_____

_____

_____

Step 5: Action—*What changes do you need to make?*

_____

_____

_____

Biblical Issues in the Church Family

Lesson 42 • Relationship with the World

Step 1: Observe—*What is written in the Bible?*

Romans 12:1, 2; 13:1-7; 1 Timothy 2:1-8; Titus 2:1-15; 3:1-14; Colossians 4:2-6; 1 Peter 3:8-17

Step 2: Respond—*What are your insights?*

What common set of guidelines can every church follow for its relationship with the world?

_____

_____

How do these guidelines for its relationship with the world enhance the concept of the church being structured as a family?

_____

_____

_____

Step 3: Discuss—*What are our shared insights?*

Is the church following or ignoring these guidelines?

_____

What problems might arise if these family guidelines for its relationship with the world are replaced with the world's business trends and organizational guidelines?

_____

_____

_____

Step 4: Summarize—*Write the key principles.*

Based on your understanding of what the Bible teaches about the church's relationship with the world, write a brief summary of the key principles that every church could follow at any time, in any culture.

_____

_____

_____

Step 5: Action—*What changes do you need to make?*

_____

_____

_____

Project J • Keeping the Church Family in Order

1. Write the biblical guidelines for each of the twelve *Biblical Issues in the Church Family* lessons and their implications for today (Lessons 31–42, pages 90–101).

_____

_____

_____

_____

_____

_____

_____

_____

_____

_____

_____

_____

_____

2. Compare your church with your outline (above). Where does your church need to change?

_____

_____

_____

_____

_____

3. What can you do to help make that happen?

_____

_____

_____

_____

4. Write a brief strategy of your role and responsibility in your family.

_____

_____

_____

_____

Part 6

Our Challenge
Develop a Church Planting Strategy

Part 6
Our Challenge: Develop a Church Planting Strategy

Project K • Design a Church Planting Strategy

Using the timeless and supra-cultural principles we have studied from the Bible, design a strategy for fully establishing a church from start to finish in your culture.

I. Church Evangelizing

A. Being Sent

    1.

    2.

    3.

    4.

B. Proclaiming the Gospel

    1.

    2.

    3.

    4.

C. Baptizing Believers

    1.

    2.

II. Church Establishing

A. In the Gospel of Faith

    1.

    2.

    3.

    4.

B. Ordered Households

    1.

    2.

    3.

    4.

C. Faithful Men

    1.

    2.

    3.

    4.

III. Church Equipping

A. Men

1.

2.

3.

4.

B. Women

1.

2.

3.

4.

C. Children

1.

2.

3.

4.

IV. Church Expanding

A. Locally

1.

2.

3.

4.

5.

B. Other Nations (people groups)

1.

2.

3.

4.

5.

See Supplement P: *Process for Starting New Churches (page 154)*

Project L • Refining Your Personal Church Planting Strategy

Using the timeless and supra-cultural principles we have studied from the Bible, develop and record a ten-year strategy God has given you for church planting. Refer to Project C (page 38) as a guideline. Your strategy will reflect the outline from Project K (page 105). Your strategy might involve time increments, geographical locations, and people groups. Use separate sheets of paper to record your strategy. Give a copy of this strategy to your mentor.

I. Church Evangelizing

    A. Being Sent

    B. Proclaiming the Gospel

    C. Baptizing Believers

II. Church Establishing

    A. In the Gospel of Faith

    B. Ordered Households

    C. Faithful Men

III. Church Equipping

    A. Men

    B. Women

    C. Children

IV. Church Expanding

    A. Locally

    B. Other Nations (people groups)

See Supplement P: *Process for Starting New Churches (page 154)*

Project M • Process for Establishing an Existing Church

What changes would you need to make in your personal church planting strategy if you were asked to go in and establish an existing church?

_____

_____

_____

_____

_____

_____

_____

_____

_____

_____

_____

_____

_____

_____

_____

_____

_____

_____

See Supplement Q: *Process for Strengthening Existing Churches (page 155)*

Church Planter's Profile

Name: _____

Wife: _____

Children: _____

_____

Location: _____

People group or groups: _____

Population of location: _____

Length of stay at location: _____

Who is your "Paul" or accountability partner? _____

Who are your "Timothys"? _____

Name of your sending church family: _____

```
                           Picture
```

Church Planter's Progress Evaluation

	Yes	No
Evangelizing		
1. Preaching the Gospel	❑	❑
2. Finding Key People	❑	❑
3. Baptizing Believers	❑	❑
Establishing		
4. Strengthening Their Faith	❑	❑
5. Setting Families in Order	❑	❑
6. Setting the Church in Order	❑	❑
7. Developing Faithful Men	❑	❑
8. Elders	❑	❑
9. Timothys'	❑	❑
Equipping		
10. Appointing Elders	❑	❑
11. Older Men Teaching Younger Men	❑	❑
12. Older Women Teaching Younger Women	❑	❑
Expanding		
13. Locally: Reproducing Churches	❑	❑
14. Other Nations: Unreached People Groups	❑	❑

Prayer Requests:

1. _____

2. _____

3. _____

4. _____

Supplements

Supplement A: *Maps of Paul's Missionary Journeys*

Paul's First Missionary Journey

Acts 13:4–14:28 • Circa A.D. 46–48

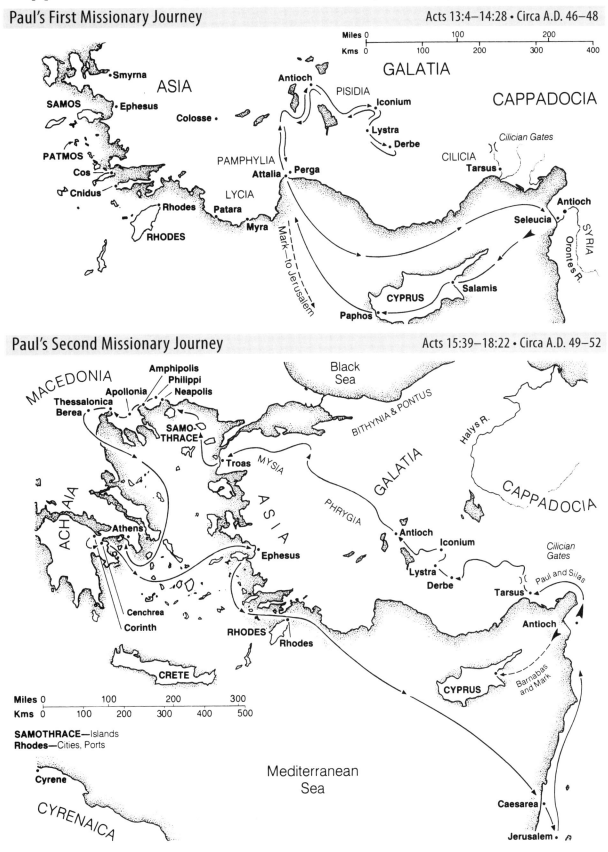

Paul's Second Missionary Journey

Acts 15:39–18:22 • Circa A.D. 49–52

SAMOTHRACE—Islands
Rhodes—Cities, Ports

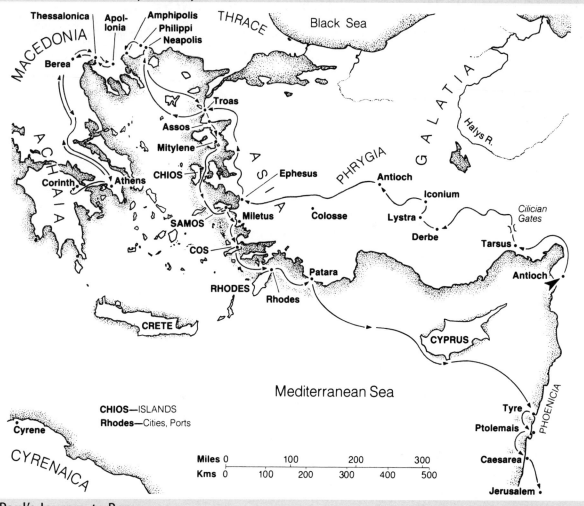

THRACE
Black Sea

MACEDONIA
Thessalonica
Apol-
Ionia
Amphipolis
Philippi
Neapolis
Berea

ACHAIA

Troas
Assos
Mitylene

CHIOS
Ephesus
PHRYGIA
Antioch
GALATIA
Halys R.

Corinth
Athens

ASIA
Iconium
Colosse
Lystra
Cilician
Gates

Miletus
SAMOS
Derbe
Tarsus

COS
Antioch

Patara
RHODES
Rhodes

CRETE

Mediterranean Sea

Tyre
PHOENICIA
Ptolemais

Caesarea

Jerusalem

CHIOS—ISLANDS
Rhodes—Cities, Ports

Cyrene

CYRENAICA

Miles	0		100		200		300	
Kms	0	100	200	300	400	500		

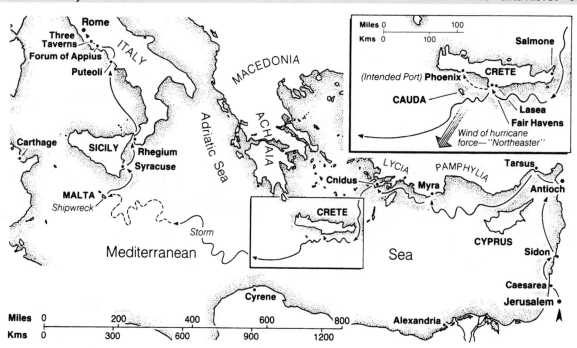

Rome
Three
Taverns
Forum of Appius
ITALY
Puteoli

MACEDONIA

Carthage
SICILY
Rhegium
Syracuse

Adriatic Sea

ACHAIA

MALTA
Shipwreck

Storm

Mediterranean

CRETE

Sea

Miles	0		100	
Kms	0	100		

Salmone

(Intended Port) Phoenix
CRETE

CAUDA
Lasea
Fair Havens

Wind of hurricane
force—"Northeaster"

Cnidus
LYCIA
PAMPHYLIA
Tarsus
Myra
Antioch

CYPRUS
Sidon

Caesarea
Jerusalem

Cyrene
Alexandria

Miles	0		200		400		600		800
Kms	0	300		600		900		1200	

Supplement B: *Returning to the Scriptures*

Church planters today may have gained a greater number of converts than Paul, but unfortunately, few have established growing churches like Paul did. Church planters have wandered from place to place without any biblical plan or strategy. Although Paul was a master church planter, present day missions, for the most part, have neither understood nor practiced his method of church planting.

Now, some might say, "Things were different in Paul's day." Did his situation contribute to greater success or was it a hindrance? Let us take a look at Paul's situation.

Paul's converts were born and bred in similar social environments as we see today in India, China, and the world in general. In Paul's days, human sacrifice was common and belief in witchcraft and demons was universal. It was the Spirit of Christ that enabled Christians to banish these demons from their hearts. Deliverance came not by denial, but by conquest. By preaching the supremacy of Christ in the power of the Holy Spirit, Paul gave the new followers of Christ the real victory! So, it is impossible to argue that Paul's converts had any social advantage over our societies today.

Think of Paul's model of establishing a church like the model of a table. It needs four strong legs to hold it up. Let's look at the legs Paul used.

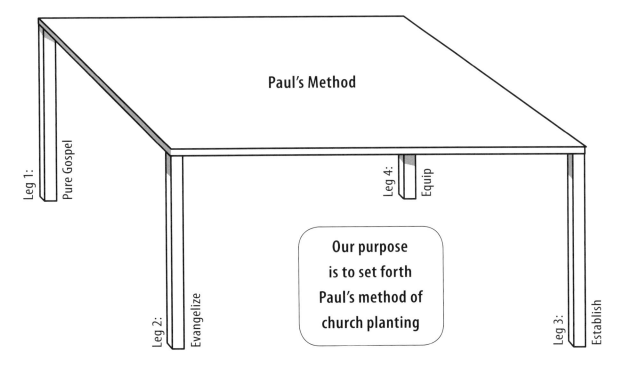

Paul's Method

Leg 1: Pure Gospel

Leg 2: Evangelize

Leg 3: Establish

Leg 4: Equip

Our purpose is to set forth Paul's method of church planting

Leg 1: Pure Gospel–Paul preached Christ and Christ crucified—the power of the Gospel unto salvation. His supreme subject was the Cross along with repentance and faith, not philosophy or psychology. There was always an air of expectation pervading his preaching. His message stood alone. If people rejected him, he moved on to find more receptive hearts—a place where God was at work.

Leg 2: Evangelize–Paul's ultimate method of evangelizing was not to preach to every person in every area by himself. His goal was to establish churches that displayed the life of Christ in key areas. From there the knowledge of Christ might be spread into the surrounding country. His design was that these key centers of intellectual and commercial activity would become sources from which the gospel would be spread in every direction.

Such strategic locations exist today. Are we utilizing them in our evangelistic strategies?

Leg 3: Establish–Paul did not seek financial help for himself, neither did he require monetary gain from those to whom he preached. Paul supported himself by the labor of his own hands and directed others to follow his example. He did not take financial support to his converts (the only exception being when he helped the starving believers in Jerusalem). He was very careful to avoid any appearance of financial profiting or misappropriation of funds. Because of this, the churches quickly became independent and self-sustaining. These churches learned to share generously among themselves and to depend on God for provision.

Leg 4: Equip–Normally Paul preached in a place for five or six months and then left behind as he traveled on an indigenous church capable of growth and expansion. Paul left his fledgling churches with a simple system of Gospel teaching: two sacraments, **a tradition of the facts of the death and resurrection of Christ**, and the Old Testament. He left no fixed standard for meetings or gatherings (services or prayer). In six months, Paul orally taught the common people and slaves (who generally were unable to read) to use the Old Testament. The simplicity and brevity of his teaching constituted its strength. By his leaving, the church was forced to think, speak, and serve. Although they were not totally free from the need for guidance and growth. Paul trained them like Jesus trained His disciples: by example and teaching them to **use** what God gave them. He left scriptural qualifications for the leaders: elders and church planters. These qualifications were primarily guidelines for moral character and instructions on the proper use of the spiritual gifts. This process contained grave risks, but Paul had such faith in Christ and the Holy Spirit's indwelling the church that he did not shrink from the task.

If any missionary today established a church like this, he might be told that his methods were hopeless. Yet the facts remain clear. Paul was the most successful founder of churches that this world has ever seen.

In contrast, let's look at the legs of the table when churches are established by today's popular methods. Let's also contemplate why they fail.

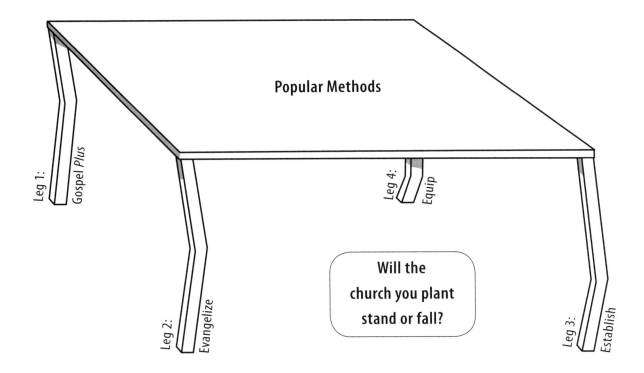

Leg 1: Gospel *Plus*—We fear rejection. Therefore, we come with programs that are seeking to be relevant and tolerant to society. The popular teachings today are often mixed with philosophy and psychology. We have forgotten that the same Lord who instructed us to "go into all the world", also gave us the command to shake the dust off our feet in places where the spiritual response is non-existent. If we continue teaching in these places, not only do we cease to preach the pure gospel, we degrade it to the level of merely educating the intellect of our audience and nothing more.

Leg 2: Evangelize—We send out teams that try to personally reach as many individuals as possible. By neglecting to use Paul's strategy of starting churches that are capable of spreading the Word, we are severely limited by what a single person or team can do. The leg that is based on separate, individual, believers lacks multiple leadership and support for spiritual growth. It is not strong enough to support a church. It will ultimately fail.

Leg 3: Establish—Today, many of our churches and mission organizations have become financial institutions rather than the body of Christ. We commonly hear they are unable to start new churches, extend their missions, or support their Bible colleges without financial assistance because of their dependence on foreign money. Foreign subsidies create foreign religious establishments that subsequently produce dependent converts who learn only to rely upon outside money instead of supplying their own needs. Traditionally the idea has been that the stability of the church depends upon the erection of a building. When we have secured a building, we tend to think a church or mission is firmly planted. In reality, buildings and money have absolutely no power to produce spiritual fruit and can actually hinder spiritual results—leaving that leg to fail.

Leg 4: Equip—Frequently, our churches are overly dependent on the one person who started that church. Often converts remain reliant upon that church planter or his successor for generations. Today, we are not training churches to use the gifts God has given them. We over emphasize the intellectual qualifications of leaders by relying heavily on artificial standards of formal education as a necessary requirement for ministry and leadership. When Paul left a church in a timely manner, it gave the church leaders the opportunity to step into their proper places and it forced the church to realize that it could not depend upon the Apostle Paul. The new church must depend upon its own resources and more importantly, upon God. If the church is left with no trained and maturing multiple leaders, that leg will fail.

Will the church you plant stand or will it fall? It depends on the legs with which you build. How will you know if the church is firmly established? You will know when it grows and reproduces like a family!

Pure Gospel + Evangelization + Establishment + Equipping Leaders | **Growth!**

What exactly happens when you are part of a growing church? It is interesting to observe that Paul's new converts became missionaries. Paul did not exhort people to enter the mission field. Naturally or supernaturally, when a person receives the Spirit, they begin to seek to bring others to the saving knowledge of Jesus. This is not surprising since the Spirit that we receive is the missionary Spirit of Jesus our Lord—the Spirit of Him who came into the world to bring lost souls to the Father. This happened in Paul's churches.

Let us observe the historical facts:

Galatia–The churches were strengthened in faith and increased in number.

Thessalonica–The Word spread to Macedonia and Achaia.

Ephesus–The gospel spread throughout neighboring countries so that many churches sprang up with members who had never even seen Paul's face.

Paul led them to the Spirit of Christ. They willingly accepted. He set them an example that was in accord with the mind of Christ. Paul was persuaded the Spirit of Christ indwelling them would enable them to *approve* the example and *inspire* them to follow the example.

A church built on broken legs cannot be firmly established. It will not grow healthy.

When the foundation of the church is not properly laid, I believe that the missionary spirit is quenched resulting in a failed church. This is yet another compelling reason to use Paul's proven method of discipleship.

Compared to Paul's established churches, today's missionary endeavors are plagued by two disquieting symptoms.

> **Strong legs=**
>
> **Indigenous and Self-sustaining**

1. We have not yet been successful in planting Christianity resulting in indigenous churches. In many countries outside of North America and Europe, Christianity is for the most part considered to be a foreign religion.

2. The missions and churches are not self-sustaining. They are unable to meet their own needs and continue to appeal for men and money. This has been a pattern for hundreds of years! The unrealistic fear is without our support, mission efforts will fail, converts will fall away, and ground that has been painfully won, will be lost.

Our mistake is that we attempt to prop up and fix the broken legs of foreign churches with money and management. We have done everything for indigenous Christians under a system of foreign leadership. We teach them and baptize them, but we continue to manage their funds, order their services and build their buildings.

Consider China, a place where Western missionaries have been forbidden, yet the church has continued to thrive and has expanded beyond measure. We do express gratitude for those pioneering and trailblazing missionaries who planted the seed and gave their lives for the gospel.

Think of it from the perspective of a teacher and a pupil. The first duty of a good teacher is not to solve all of the difficulties for the pupil or present him with a ready-made answer. Something more valuable needs to happen. The pupil needs to learn confidence in his inherited powers and spiritual gifts. Once this is accomplished, the teacher can set difficulties before him, show him how to approach problems, and how to overcome them successfully.

This is how Jesus taught His twelve disciples. This is what Paul did with his brief visits and letters. He was glad when his converts could progress without his constant aid. I believe with the help of the Holy Spirit, you also will be able to plant God's church on four strong legs. Those legs will not only support it, but sustain and advance His church.

Application: How do we follow Paul's example today?

To build the four legs of a healthy church, a church planter needs to be *timeless* and *supra-cultural*. Being timeless means that our biblical teachings are comprised of lessons that could apply to any time. Teaching supra-cultural means that we are applying biblical principles that will work for any culture. Careful scrutiny of Scripture will show you exactly what Paul did to build a church and what he taught to strengthen it. God was able to use Paul in many different places.

Absolutes

(See pages 22, 30)

Timeless	Supra-Cultural
Apply to any time	Apply to any culture

Non-Absolutes

Forms, Patterns, Organizations, Methods and Structures

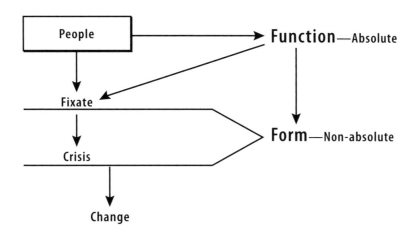

Use Hebrews 10:24-25 to contrast **absolutes** with **non-absolutes**.

Non-Absolutes	Absolutes

Note: Some information from Gene Getz, *Sharpening the Focus of the Church*.

Let's look at the four legs in light of these timeless and supra-cultural principles:

1. Pure Gospel–Paul taught the true gospel, pure and simple. He did not include popular thoughts on psychology, philosophy or politics. His message was our Lord's message: the simple, honest, light of salvation through Christ's death for us.

2. Evangelize–Paul had a plan for spreading the gospel from a few strategic locations. If you look at the maps of his missionary journeys (Supplement A, pages 115–116) his strategy will become clear. There are key locations in our world today. We can prayerfully choose these places and plan our strategy for maximum results.

3. Establish–Materially providing for a church does not mean that the church is healthy or established. The value of money is subject to change. Let each church determine its own needs and let each indigenous community supply what is necessary for its own operations.

4. Equip–Teach and appoint those who are scripturally qualified as leaders and elders. Give them the authority to exercise their spiritual gifts immediately. Give the raising and management of all local funds to the church so that its needs are met. Teach the whole community to be responsible for the proper administration of baptism, ordination and discipline. When these four steps are completed, leave.

While this last point may seem counter-productive, think of it in this way: we *never* inspire confidence and faith in the power of the Holy Spirit unless we *demonstrate* it through our actions. You, as the church planter, should be clear that your role is not permanent and that you have no successor. When you leave, the church remains because, unlike you, its people are permanent. Only by your leaving can the way be prepared for their true independence from you and their true dependence on God. I have seen new believers from the lowest castes in India understand the gospel and become capable of making disciples in less than a year after conversion.

You, the church planter, are like the bee that drops needed pollen. Without pollen, there is no fruit. Without believers, there is no church. You give them what they need—pure gospel, training and authority. Then you move on so that the maturing, growth and reproduction is able to take place. The bee's continued presence is not needed for the plant to mature, produce fruit and propagate. God has provided a plan for that to happen within the plant itself. God has provided a plan for His church to grow and we need to trust in that plan.

Supplement C: *Church Planting Movements*

First of all, it is obvious from Jesus' teachings concerning His Kingdom that He expected dramatic growth. One of the many illustrations of this is the parable of the mustard seed in Matthew 13:31-32. The mustard seed was the smallest of seeds and yet grows larger than all the other garden plants. The end result of the tiny mustard seed is an enormous tree.

Secondly, Christ seemed to indicate that the gospel was to be implanted into other cultures. Matthew 13:33 uses a word picture comparing this concept to yeast being mixed into a large amount of dough. The earliest illustration of cross-cultural evangelism is observed when we study the Jewish church quickly morphing into a Gentile church. After hundreds of years, Christianity today remains largely a foreign or western religion.

This might be one of the reasons why the spread of Christianity has been hindered.

Bob Goldman observes:

> To the extent that new believers are perceived by others as having chosen foreign identities and joined a foreign religious community, then the opportunity for the gospel to rapidly spread in the people group is dramatically diminished.

Church Planting Movements Defined:

> A rapid multiplication of indigenous churches planting churches that sweeps through a people group or population segment.

David Garrison; author of *Church Planting Movements*

> A rapid growth in the number of believers which is beyond the influence or control of the ones who introduced the gospel.

Bob Goldman; strategist with *Mission Frontiers*

Example: Mongolia and China

Church Planting Movement Accelerators

Accelerators are church planting actions that may not be measurable and may take longer to see fruit. However, these plants are more likely to become strong Christian fellowships with lasting Kingdom results. Note: One of the purposes of this church planting manual is help accelerate and sustain church planting movements. **This is accomplished by building biblical tracks for these church-planting movements to run on while laying a biblical foundation for the movements to stand on.**

Example: Early church (Acts) and West Bengal, India

Church Planting Movement Inhibitors

Inhibitors are church planting actions that may bring measurable short-term results, but are much more likely to inhibit fellowships from becoming movements of Christ with lasting results.

Example: Cambodia (Hmong) and Karnataka, India

Accelerators	Inhibitors
Communal Society	Individualistic Society
Family Conversion Patterns	Breakdown of Family Order
Churches Planting Churches	Individualistic Evangelism
Training "in" Ministry	Academic Training "for" Ministry
Cultivate and Empower Indigenous Leadership	Start with Foreign Leadership
Debt Free or Financial Independence	Debt and Financial Dependence
Christ, Head of the Church	Pastor, or Man as Head of Church
Multiple Leaders with Equality	Single Leader with Authoritative Style
Preserve Insider Identity	Establish a Foreign Identity
House Churches or Temporary Buildings	Permanent Buildings and Land
Persecution and Suffering	Ease, Pleasure, and Entertainment
Penetrate Existing Communities with Gospel	Extract Believers into New Communities
Emphasize Community-oriented Fellowship	Emphasize Meeting-oriented Church
Contextualized Worship and Sacraments	Adopt Foreign Practices for Gatherings
Preserve Local Financial Independence	Accept Foreign Money and Dependence
Leaders Tent-making, or Working for Needs	Leaders Full Financial Support
Authority and Sufficiency of God's Word	Bible Not Enough
Devotion to Prayer and Christ	Organizational and Business Practices
Godliness	Worldliness
Rapid Incorporation of New Believers	Rigid Requirements for Membership
High Cost of Following Christ	No Cost to Follow Christ
Bold, Spirit-filled, and Fearless Faith	Human Eloquence and Intellect
Releasing Disciples and Leaders	Retaining Disciples and Leaders

Add or make your own list of accelerators and inhibitors. Remember that these can and will vary from culture to culture and time to time.

Accelerators	Inhibitors

Not only is God moving in the world today....He's moving quickly. What a privilege to be part of this adventure!

—*Scott Holste and Jim Haney; Global Research*

Note: Some information from David Garrison's book, *Church Planting Movements*, and Bob Goldman's article in *Mission Frontiers*.

Supplement D: *People Groups*

(See www.finishingthetask.com)

Why Unreached People Groups?

Genesis 12:1-3

Psalms 67

Habakkuk 1:5, 2:14

Matthew 28:19-28—Making disciples of all people groups

Matthew 24:14—Testimony to all people groups

Revelation 5:9; 4:11; 5:9; 14:6; 21:24; 22:1-5—Heaven is full of ransomed people from every people group

People Groups: a large group of people through which the gospel can flow without encountering significant barriers of understanding the gospel; these barriers include language, customs, and family or clan identities.

Location of People Groups

Many unreached people groups are located in the 10/40 window which comprises one-third of the world's land and two-thirds of the world's people.

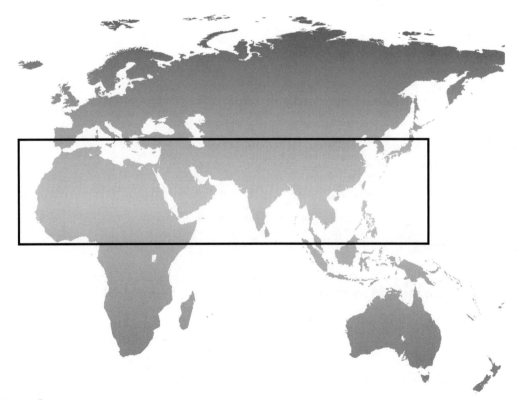

Ninety-five percent of these people have not heard the gospel.

Eighty-five percent of these people groups are among the world's poorest.

The unreached people groups are categorized into several groups by the ministry of www.peoplegroups.org.

0–No evangelical Christians or churches as well as no access to major evangelical print, audio, visual, or human resources.

1–Less than 2% evangelical with some evangelical resources available, but no active church planting within the past 2 years.

2–Less than 2% evangelical with initial (localized) church planting within the past 2 years.

3–Less than 2% evangelical with widespread church planting within the past 2 years.

Eighteen mission agencies, including four of the world's largest, are working together with churches in "Finishing the Task" (FTT) of reaching the unreached people groups. Their strategy is to nurture church-planting movements among 639 unengaged and unreached people groups numbering more than 100,000 in population. Any day the last people group could be reached thereby ushering in the coming of our Savior. What an awesome time in history to be living with this goal in reach and with opportunities abounding! Christ will build His church with or without us. Therefore, participating in making disciples of all people groups is a privilege.

Supplement E: *Map of the Spread of the Gospel*

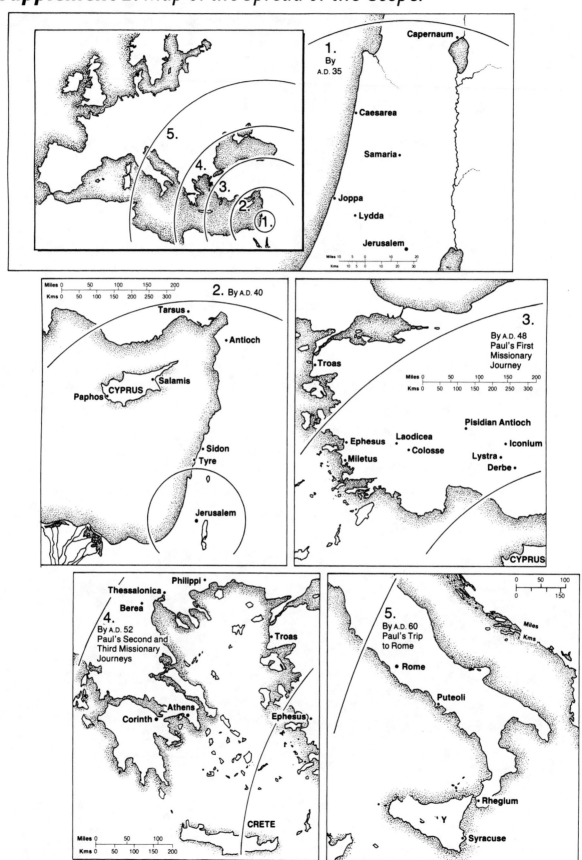

Supplement F: *Factors that Made the Early Church Powerful*

I. Introduction

What factors made the early church so dynamic and powerful? How can these factors be restored and used to impact our community and world today? The purpose of this study is to identify the factors that made the early church dynamic and to suggest practical ways that those factors can be restored in us today.

II. God Chooses

A. Those we might think unlikely

Gideon in leading the nation of Israel: "I am the least in my father's house," Judges 6:11-16.

David was the last child born to Jesse, 1 Samuel 16:6-11.

Peter and John, unlearned and ignorant men, but they had been with Jesus, Acts 4:13-14.

Paul was ordained to be an apostle and claimed to be the least of the apostles, not worthy to be called; not many mighty, not many noble called, but God chose foolish, 1 Corinthians 1:16-30.

B. Those filled with the Holy Spirit (Acts 2:4; 4:8; 9:17; 13:52)

C. Five important phases of experiencing the power of the Holy Spirit

1. Indwelt: To be indwelt by the Holy Spirit. The indwelling takes place at salvation, Romans 8:16; 1 Corinthians 12:13.

2. Filled: As believers, we are commanded to be filled with the Spirit, Ephesians 5:18 (present tense, continuous action). Where? Since the Spirit already indwells our spirit, it relates to our soul (mind, will, and emotions).

3. Yield: We are to yield our members as servants to righteousness and holiness, not uncleanness and iniquity, Romans 6:19.

4. Testing: Then Holy Spirit will direct us into a time of testing which should result in obedience and rejoicing in the Word of God, 1 Thessalonians 1:5,6.

5. Obedience or Passing: We will be empowered for service, Acts 5:32.

D. The Apostles follow Jesus' example

The Apostles were given a test of obedience followed by the power of the Spirit on the day of Pentecost. The same pattern was seen in the life of Christ. He was filled with the Spirit at His baptism and then led by the Spirit into testing. He returned in the power of the Spirit and fame of His ministry spread throughout the entire region.

Jesus carefully trained and prepared His disciples to experience this power so His church could impact the world.

Jesus illustrates a four-fold sequence in His life and ministry:

1. Filled with Holy Spirit at baptism, Matthew 3:16,17.

2. Led by the Spirit into the wilderness to face test, Matthew 4:1.

3. Passed test by quoting Scripture, Matthew 4:3-11.

4. He returned in the power of Spirit for ministry, Matthew 4:17.

III. God Tests Us to Use Us

A. Examples:

Adam: Genesis 2-3

Moses: Numbers 20

Nation of Israel: Deuteronomy

Joshua: Joshua

Gideon: Judges 6-8

Early Churches: Acts

Thessalonian believers

Apostle Paul

B. What kind of tests might be experienced? (2 Corinthians 12:8-11)

Infirmities: Physical disease or sickness

Reproaches: Insults, verbal injury or abuse, slander, gossip

Necessities: Fulfilling personal and work responsibilities

Persecutions: One stalks his victim and creates trouble

Distresses: Afflictions, anguish, grief and great sorrow

C. Why are we tested? (2 Corinthians 12:10-11)

1. Paul understood that through trials we would experience the power of the Holy Spirit. Therefore we should gladly received and even take pleasure in trials, 2 Corinthians 12:10.

2. Tests were given to Paul so that more power could come upon his life. Once Paul understood this great truth, he eagerly embraced his infirmity and in fact, gloried in it and thanked God for it.

IV. God's Power

A. The power to do greater things! (John 14:12)

Sounds incredible. What could be more incredible than giving sight to the blind, causing the deaf to hear, cleansing lepers, feeding the thousands, raising the dead? The greatest work in the world is for God's Spirit to transform cold, hard, unrepentant hearts into loving, forgiving worshipers of Christ.

It is this loving power of the Holy Spirit flowing through the yielded, obedient believer that has the capability of being used to turn men's hearts to the Lord and redeeming their souls for all eternity.

B. How to pass the test?

When the test comes, like first century Christians, rejoice in the hope of experiencing the power of the Holy Spirit, James 1:2; 1 Peter 1:6,7.

But Satan loves to take trials that God allows for increasing power, and instead, get us to murmur and complain about them. This is precisely what happened to the nation of Israel. **Moses** made it clear that the murmuring was against God, not Moses or Aaron. **Paul** pointed out that if the believer fails to rejoice and give thanks in trials, he will turn authority over to Satan for physical and spiritual destruction.

V. Your Tests Results

A. Fail:

Anger, complaining, bitterness, wilderness experience, zero power, defeat.

B. Pass:

Power, maturity, thankfulness, joy, fruitfulness, victory!

Supplement G: *Overview of the Book of Acts*

Acts: Book of History

Purpose/Theme:

The physician Luke is generally accepted as the author of this record of the establishment and growth of the early church. It emphasized the presence of the Holy Spirit, the missionary work of Peter and Paul, and how Christianity was not the enemy of the Roman government.

Key Verse:

"But you will receive power when the Holy Spirit comes on you; and you will be my witnesses in Jerusalem, and in all Judea and Samaria, and to the ends of the earth." (Acts 1:8)

Outline:

The gospel is preached

- in Jerusalem (Acts 1–7)

- in Judea and Samaria (Acts 8–12)

- to the world (Acts 13–28)

Timeline of Major Events:

30 AD			35 AD	
Ascension	Pentecost	Persecution of Apostles	Saul (Paul)	Peter

45 AD	48 AD	50 AD	52 AD	53 AD	57 AD	60 AD
First Missionary Journey		Second Missionary Journey		Third Missionary Journey	Shipwreck	Letters

Supplement H: Church Planter's Support

Tent-making Versus Full Support

To make tents or not to make tents? The question has relevance to church planters, not only because it is a biblical norm, but because more and more tent-makers are getting involved in the work of church planting. One must realize that if church planters are receiving the bulk of their income from donor gifts, then they are forfeiting their ability to be an example to the majority of believers.

I. Paul, the Model Church Planter

Look at the **model church planter**, the Apostle Paul. He was the greatest church planter who ever lived, yet he deliberately chose to work with his hands. With all his apostolic authority and connections with the churches Paul probably could have received full financial support, but he supported himself and his team of ministry companions. Paul's model of working appears to have helped advance the gospel, rather than hinder its progress.

II. Paul Showed Them (Acts 20:33-35)

Paul's example to the Ephesian elders is very clear: "I have not coveted anyone's silver or gold or clothing. You yourselves know that these hands of mine have supplied my own needs and the needs of my companions. In everything I did, I **showed you that by this kind of hard work** we must help the weak, remembering the words the Lord Jesus, 'It is more blessed to give than to receive'" (Acts 20:33-35 NIV).

III. Paul Made Himself a Model (2 Thessalonians 3:7-13)

Another example was to the Thessalonians: "For you yourselves know how you ought to follow our example. We were not idle when we were with you, nor did we eat anyone's food without paying for it. On the contrary, we worked night and day, laboring and toiling so that we would not be a burden to any of you. We did this, not because we do not have the right to such help, but in order to **make ourselves a model for you to follow**. For even when we were with you, we gave you this rule: 'If a man will not work, he shall not eat.' We hear that some among you are idle. They are not busy; they are busybodies. Such people we command and urge in the Lord Jesus Christ to settle down and earn the bread they eat. And as for you brothers, never tire of doing what is right" (2 Thessalonians 3:7-13 NIV).

IV. Paul Won the Respect of Outsiders (1 Thessalonians 4:11-12)

Even in Paul's first letter to the Thessalonians, he is concerned about his example: "Make it your ambition to lead a quiet life, to mind your own business and to work with your hands, just as we told you, so that your daily life may **win the respect of outsiders and so** that you will not be dependent on anybody" (1 Thessalonians 4:11-12 NIV).

V. Paul Gave Up His Right (1 Corinthians 9)

1 Corinthians chapter 9 contains one of the most direct discussions on the question of paid church planters found in the New Testament. Paul defends, with four arguments, his right as an apostle to be supported by those among whom he travels (verses 1-6). He argues from human experience (verse 7), the Old Testament agricultural law (verses 8-10; Deuteronomy 25:4), the practice of other workers (verses 11-12), and Old Testament Levitical custom (verse 13). But, Paul explicitly gives up this right in order to minister more effectively (verses 15-23) recognizing that the real reward is a spiritual inheritance yet to come (verses 24-27). Paul explains that he wants to **make the gospel of Christ available without charge** (verse 18).

VI. Paul Wanted an Effective Ministry (2 Corinthians 7–12)

Paul did not want to be misunderstood or have the effectiveness of his ministry reduced. That is why Paul did not normally receive money from those he was presently ministering to (2 Corinthians 7:2-4; 11:20-21; 12:14-15, etc). He was willing to receive gifts after he had left, as in Philippi. Paul was willing to labor in accordance with God's provision; making tents or receiving support from others (Philippians 4:10-14). Regardless, **Paul was content and free.**

VII. The Church Planter Norm

Those men who are completely financially supported need to realize that they have a limited ministry with respect to setting a good example for future leaders. The ideal model is the type of committed church planter who will serve as a model to all the members of the assemblies as he balances the responsibilities of family, job, and ministry. The **self-supporting church planter** should be the norm in a reproducing model of church life, although he is free to receive support or work.

VIII. Who Will Be That One Man?

It is almost universally taken for granted that credible missionary work is the work of a paid professional who trains up indigenous leaders who think they must be fully supported. Westerners have carried this philosophy all over the world as if it were an essential part of the gospel.

The expansion of the church, reduced to its elements, is a very simple thing. It asks for no elaborate organization, no large finances, and no great numbers of paid missionaries. In its new beginning it may be the work of one man who is neither learned in things of this world nor rich in the wealth of this world. Rather, it is one who has been with Jesus and is full of the Holy Spirit!

Supplement I: Church Planter's Ministry Described Biblically

The ministry of church planters or apostles (with a small "a") did not end in the first century. Today they are often referred to as "missionaries" or "evangelists," or even "pastors." But do modern day definitions go far enough in explaining this New Testament calling and ministry? They were an extension of the church, whose ministry included **preaching** the gospel, **teaching** converts, forming, caring and **establishing** the churches. This will look familiar as the process of Evangelizing, Establishing, Equipping and Expanding.

The Church Planter's Ministry Described

Evangelizing:

The church planters founded the church by **preaching the gospel** and organizing believers into community based groups. The teachings that formed the believer's faith were the foundation of the church. At times, the church planters would have to do repair work on this foundation.

Establishing:

He was to be devoted to establishing churches, **setting them in order** through teaching and preaching the truths of how a church, the household of God, ought to conduct itself. This was all done with a view of keeping the church on course (Titus 1:5; 1 Timothy 3:14-16; 6:2d; 1 Thessalonians 2:1–3:10).

Equipping:

He **appointed elders** or pastors and entrusted them with the nurture of those who had been brought in while he went on to other places. His nature of ministry made it necessary that he should be able, also, to act at times as a pastor/elder (I Peter 5:1; 2 John 1:1; 3 John 1:1) in order to establish new churches. However, he never settled down anywhere to do the work of a local pastor/elder. Not only was he involved in the recognizing and appointing of elders, it was necessary for him to confront elders who were sinning (Acts 20:17-38, especially verses 31-32; 2 Timothy 2:2; 3:1-7; 5:17-25; Titus 1:2-9).

Expanding:

He was to give priority time to **developing faithful "Timothy's;"** younger, godly men to whom he could **pass on** the Scriptures (2 Timothy 2:2). He was the extension agent, the missionary who was **responsible for planting and establishing the churches**.

The Church Planter's Instructions Given

Paul's Instruction:

The church planter's instruction is given in Paul's letters to Timothy and Titus. They deal with the church planter's life and ministry. A veteran missionary, Paul is giving practical advice to the young church planter, Timothy.

Godliness:

He is to **pay close attention to his own life and teaching, training and disciplining himself for the purpose of godliness,** so that his progress is evident to all. He was to work hard like a farmer, be disciplined as an athlete, and be as untangled in civilian life as a soldier (1 Timothy 4:1-16; 2 Timothy 2:3-6).

Preparedness:

Paul knew the roughness of the road, the hardness of the fight, the subtlety of the enemy, the special dangers and temptations that beset the church planter, and the need for constant vigilance and readiness.

The Church Planter's Authority

Authority:

Their charge and authority comes from God. Their work is to preach and teach in season and out (2 Timothy 4:1-5); (Titus 2), to establish churches (Titus 1:5; Acts 14:23), to oversee churches and elders (1 Timothy 1:3; Titus 1:5; 1 Timothy 4:11-13; 5:1, 17, 19-20; 2 Timothy 4:2-5; Titus 2), to reprove, rebuke, exhort (1 Timothy 5:20-21; Titus1:13-14; 2:15), guard against doctrines of demons and refute those who contradict (Titus 3:10-11; Acts 15:1-2; 1 Timothy 1:3-4) and to minister through prayer and faith (2 Timothy 4:1-4; 2:22-26; 1 Timothy 4:1-16). Their preparation, under the providential guidance of the Holy Spirit, is to study the Scriptures to obtain experiential knowledge by participating in the life and work of the local churches.

The Church Planter's Call Confirmed

Confirmation:

His call was received directly from the Lord and made known to the leaders by the Holy Spirit (Acts 13:2-4; 16:1-3). This is beautifully described in Acts 13:2, "While they were worshiping the Lord and fasting, the Holy Spirit said, 'Set apart for me Barnabas and Saul for the work to which I have called them.'"

The leaders, having received from the Holy Spirit the confirmation of an evangelist's call, associated itself with him by the laying on of hands (1 Timothy 4:1-4; 2 Timothy 1:6; Acts 13:2-3). Where would he go? He was to be available to minister locally and in other parts of the world as God would open doors and confirm through the leaders God has placed over him. This should primarily mean taking the gospel to new areas and establishing new churches, or further establishing existing churches (Acts 13:1–14:26; 15:36–16:5; Philippians 1:3-7; 2:19-24; 1 Thessalonians 1:1-3: 13; 1 Timothy 3:14-16; Titus 1:5).

The Church Planter's Teamwork

Teams:

Apostles usually ministered in and with **"apostolic teams."** These teams do not have authority over the local church elders who have been charged to shepherd the flock of God, nor are they under the authority of the elders. Rather we believe they were in complementary relationships. They functioned as part of the shepherding team, alongside the elders, when they resided in one local church for a period of time.

The apostles served as links among the existing churches and were also involved in starting and helping establish new churches. Several of the "other apostles" mentioned in the Scriptures were Andronicus, Apollos, Barnabas, Epaphras, Epaphroditus, Junias, Justus, Silas, Timothy, Titus, and Tychicus.

Mentoring:

There is a multiply component—not only in seeing churches reproduce, but also to get **teams to reproduce**. I believe God is still calling "wise master builders" to serve not only in planting the church but also as mentors to younger teams of church planters.

The Church Planter's Responsibilities

The **"kind of men they were"** provided a powerful validation of the truths they were teaching to those listening. They were men who were passionate about maintaining a clear conscience before both God and men (1 Thessalonians 1:5; 2:3, 10).

They **preached the gospel** to the unsaved and established new churches when those who heard their message repented from their sin and believed (Acts 13:1-28; Colossians 1:7).

They served as a communication **link between the churches** and the apostle Paul and others exchanged information and reports. They were also itinerant laborers in that they traveled among the churches and stayed from a few months to a few years (Acts 14:27; 20:31; Colossians 4:7-18).

They **encouraged the hearts of the saints** through teaching, exhorting and admonishing them in the Word. By living among the people they became "living epistles" (1 Thessalonians 1:1-9).

They **"set in order what remained"** in newly founded churches by seeing to their needs, appointing elders and teaching and training them and the church in the whole counsel of God (Acts 20:25-38; Titus 1:5).

They **worked day and night with their own hands** to support their needs financially. In doing so they set an example for the saints that "it is more blessed to give than to receive." (Acts 20:35 NIV) This removed the possibility of people thinking they were being manipulated for the sake of financial gain by those proclaiming the gospel. They were in effect 'tent-makers.' They were occasionally supported by churches, but not a church where they were currently ministering. Several times it appears that they refused support (Acts 20:33-38; 1 Thessalonians 1:1-9; 2 Thessalonians 3).

They helped **resolve serious conflict** within the churches and confronted sin (Acts 15:1-41; Galatians 2:11-14; 2 Timothy 2:24-26).

Supplement J: *Timeline of Paul's Ministry and Letters*

A.D. 5
Birth of Saul

Between 6 B.C. and A.D. 10,
but probably about A.D. 5
(based on the terms "young man,"
Acts 7:58 and "old man," Phil 9).

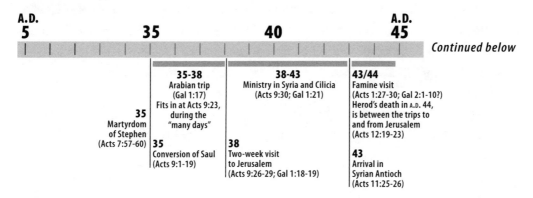

A.D.
5 .... **35** .... **40** .... **A.D. 45**   *Continued below*

35-38
Arabian trip
(Gal 1:17)
Fits in at Acts 9:23,
during the
"many days"

35
Martyrdom
of Stephen
(Acts 7:57-60)

35
Conversion of Saul
(Acts 9:1-19)

38-43
Ministry in Syria and Cilicia
(Acts 9:30; Gal 1:21)

38
Two-week visit
to Jerusalem
(Acts 9:26-29; Gal 1:18-19)

43/44
Famine visit
(Acts 1:27-30; Gal 2:1-10?)
Herod's death in A.D. 44,
is between the trips to
and from Jerusalem
(Acts 12:19-23)

43
Arrival in
Syrian Antioch
(Acts 11:25-26)

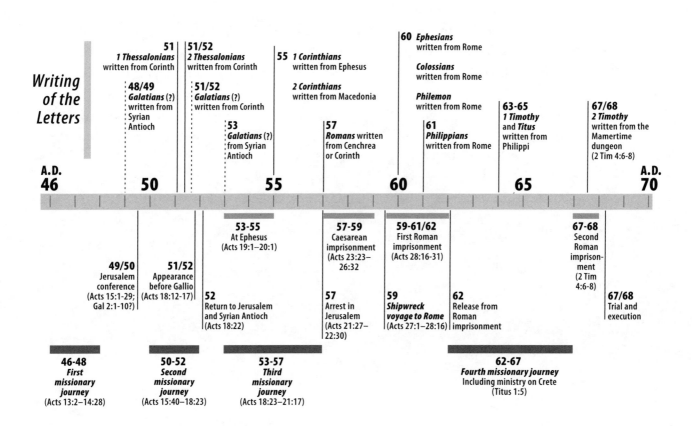

*Writing
of the
Letters*

51
1 Thessalonians
written from Corinth

48/49
Galatians (?)
written from
Syrian
Antioch

51/52
2 Thessalonians
written from Corinth

51/52
Galatians (?)
written from
Corinth

53
Galatians (?)
from Syrian
Antioch

55 *1 Corinthians*
written from Ephesus

2 Corinthians
written from Macedonia

57
Romans written
from Cenchrea
or Corinth

60 *Ephesians*
written from Rome

Colossians
written from Rome

Philemon
written from Rome

61
Philippians
written from Rome

63-65
1 Timothy
and *Titus*
written from
Philippi

67/68
2 Timothy
written from the
Mamertime
dungeon
(2 Tim 4:6-8)

A.D.
46 ...... **50** .... **55** .... **60** .... **65** .... **A.D. 70**

53-55
At Ephesus
(Acts 19:1–20:1)

57-59
Caesarean
imprisonment
(Acts 23:23–
26:32)

59-61/62
First Roman
imprisonment
(Acts 28:16-31)

67-68
Second
Roman
imprison-
ment
(2 Tim
4:6-8)

49/50
Jerusalem
conference
(Acts 15:1-29;
Gal 2:1-10?)

51/52
Appearance
before Gallio
(Acts 18:12-17)

52
Return to Jerusalem
and Syrian Antioch
(Acts 18:22)

57
Arrest in
Jerusalem
(Acts 21:27–
22:30)

59
*Shipwreck
voyage to Rome*
(Acts 27:1–28:16)

62
Release from
Roman
imprisonment

67/68
Trial and
execution

46-48
*First
missionary
journey*
(Acts 13:2–14:28)

50-52
*Second
missionary
journey*
(Acts 15:40–18:23)

53-57
*Third
missionary
journey*
(Acts 18:23–21:17)

62-67
Fourth missionary journey
Including ministry on Crete
(Titus 1:5)

Supplement K: *Effects of Not Being Established*

Paul's Letters to the Churches

Paul's Early Letters to the Church

Desire to Establish Young Churches in the Gospel	Effects of Not Being Fully Established in the Gospel
Galatians: • Returning to the pure gospel, not mixing it with the Law	**Galatians:** • Legalism and hypocrisy, a spying attitude towards others • Critical, jealous and angry spirit towards others
1 & 2 Thessalonians: • Standing firm in the gospel	**1 & 2 Thessalonians:** • Doctrinal rabbit trails • Future things • Irresponsible lifestyles
1 Corinthians: • Divisions solved by the implications of the gospel **2 Corinthians:** • Defense of the ministry of the gospel	**1 & 2 Corinthians:** • Divisions in the church—seen in disputes and suits, in marriages, in matters of personal preference, in pitting leaders against each other • Rejection of those who are correcting and exhorting; listening to those who undermine them
Romans: • Preaching a complete treatise of the gospel	**Romans:** • Failure to become free of life-controlling problems

Paul's Letters Written from Prison

Desire For Churches to be One-Minded Concerning Person and Plan of Christ	Effects of Not Being Fully Established in the Gospel
Ephesians: • Grasping the mystery of the church • Focusing on the plan of Christ	**Ephesians:** • No sense of corporate power • Inability to stand against schemes of the devil • Parts not contributing to the whole body
Philippians: • One minded participation as a church in the progress of the gospel	**Philippians:** • Lack of one-mindedness for the progression of the gospel • Lack of striving together as a body
Colossians: • Grasping the mystery of the church • Focusing on the head of the church	**Colossians:** • Embracing another philosophy with different principles and a focus different than Christ • Mind set on earthly things resulting in disharmony in the church and home
Philemon: • Relational implications of one-minded participation in the progress of the gospel	**Philemon:** • Failure to accept wrongs done to us for the benefit of progressing the gospel

Paul's Final Set of Pastoral Letters

Desire For Churches to be Properly Ordered Households of God	Effects of Not Being Fully Established in the Gospel
1 Timothy: • Properly ordering the community life of the 'household of God', the church of Jesus Christ	**1 Timothy:** • Inability to avoid deceitful spirits and doctrines of demons • Confusion of roles of men and women of the church
Titus: • Setting in order what remains • Fully establishing the churches by teaching sound doctrine	**Titus:** • Confusion in families • Confusion of roles and functions • Lives that dishonor the Word of God rather than admiring the gospel • Foolish controversies replacing good deeds
2 Timothy: • The significance and function of well trained, faithful leaders	**2 Timothy:** • People pursuing teachers that tell them what they want to hear • People falling away from the faith

Supplement L: *Qualifications for Elders*

As to God and His Word

Not a new convert (1 Timothy 3:6). Do you truly know the Lord and are you in a continual progress in spiritual maturity and growth?

Dissatisfied   1   2   3   4   5   6   7   Satisfied

Devout (Titus 1:8). Do you demonstrate a definite commitment to know, love, and walk with God?

Dissatisfied   1   2   3   4   5   6   7   Satisfied

Holding fast to the faithful Word . . . able to exhort . . . and refute . . . (1 Timothy 3:2; Titus 1:9). Do you have that quality of life and biblical knowledge that enables you to communicate the Word of God to others effectively maintaining a gentle attitude.

Dissatisfied   1   2   3   4   5   6   7   Satisfied

As to Himself

If a man aspires to the office of overseer (1 Timothy 3:1). Do you have a compelling desire to serve the Lord and the body of Christ as an overseer of the flock, not under compulsion but voluntarily?

Dissatisfied   1   2   3   4   5   6   7   Satisfied

Temperate (1 Timothy 3:2). In daily life, do you tend to react under the Spirit's control according to biblical principles?

Dissatisfied   1   2   3   4   5   6   7   Satisfied

Prudent (1 Timothy 3:2). Do you have a correct view of yourself in relationship to God and other Christians?

Dissatisfied   1   2   3   4   5   6   7   Satisfied

Not quick tempered (Titus 1:7). Do you have a short fuse? Do you harbor feelings of resentment over a period of time?

Dissatisfied   1   2   3   4   5   6   7   Satisfied

As to His Family

Husband of one wife (1 Timothy 3:2; Titus 1:6). How is your relationship with your wife? Literally, are you a one-woman man?

Dissatisfied   1   2   3   4   5   6   7   Satisfied

One who manages his own household well (1 Timothy 3:4-5; Titus 1:6). Do your wife and children love, respect, and follow your leadership and are they responding to your God and His claim on their lives?

Dissatisfied   1   2   3   4   5   6   7   Satisfied

As to Others

Hospitable (1 Timothy 3:2; Titus 1:8). Literally, are you "a lover of strangers" and do you use your home as a means to minister to others?

Dissatisfied   1   2   3   4   5   6   7   Satisfied

Able to teach (1 Timothy 3:2). Are you able to communicate the Word of God to others and handle those who disagree with you in a patient and gentle manner? Do others recognize your ability to teach and communicate the Word?

Dissatisfied   1   2   3   4   5   6   7   Satisfied

Not self-willed (Titus 1:7). Do you always have to have your own way or do you set aside your own preferences in order to promote unity and care for the needs of others?

Dissatisfied   1   2   3   4   5   6   7   Satisfied

Loving what is good (Titus 1:8). Do you desire to associate yourself with truth, honor, and integrity; and do you take advantage of opportunities to do good to all men in order to build them up rather than tear them down?

Dissatisfied   1   2   3   4   5   6   7   Satisfied

Not pugnacious or a striker, i.e., anger out of control (1 Timothy 3:3; Titus 1:7). Do you show a tendency to be either physically or verbally abusive because of angry feelings?

Dissatisfied   1   2   3   4   5   6   7   Satisfied

Contentious (1 Timothy 3:3). Do you purposely take the opposite point of view from others for self-seeking reasons such as jealousy or selfish ambition?

Dissatisfied   1   2   3   4   5   6   7   Satisfied

Gentle (1 Timothy 3:3). Are you yielding, showing gentleness and kindness; or are you heavy-handed, insisting on the letter of the law?

Dissatisfied   1   2   3   4   5   6   7   Satisfied

Just (Titus 1:8). Are you able to make just decisions, those that are wise, fair, impartial, objective, and honest according to Scripture?

Dissatisfied   1   2   3   4   5   6   7   Satisfied

Respectable, orderly, balanced (1 Timothy 3:2). Are you respected by others because your life adorns the Word of God in a blended and balanced manner?

Dissatisfied   1   2   3   4   5   6   7   Satisfied

Having a good reputation with those on the outside (1 Timothy 1:7). Do you have a good reputation among unbelievers because you have a lifestyle of unquestioned integrity?

Dissatisfied   1   2   3   4   5   6   7   Satisfied

As to Things

Free from the love of money (1 Timothy 3:3; Titus 1:7). Do you seek significance, security, and primary satisfaction from material wealth? Do you seek His kingdom and His righteousness first?

Dissatisfied   1   2   3   4   5   6   7   Satisfied

Not addicted to wine (1 Timothy 3:3; Titus 1:7). Are you free from any kind of addiction which might take control of your life or cause weaker Christians to stumble (Romans 14:13-21)?

Dissatisfied   1   2   3   4   5   6   7   Satisfied

Supplement M: *Qualifications for Deacons*

In General

Tested . . . beyond reproach (1 Timothy 3:10). Having been observed over a period of time, are there any violations in the qualities needed to serve that would disqualify you as a deacon, or do you need more time?

Dissatisfied   1   2   3   4   5   6   7   Satisfied

As to God and His Word

Holding to the mystery of the faith with a clear conscience (1 Timothy 3:8). "The mystery of the faith" refers to the body of Christian doctrine with a clear conscience? Do you keep a clear conscience before God?

Dissatisfied   1   2   3   4   5   6   7   Satisfied

As to Self

Men of dignity (1 Timothy 3:8). Do you take your life and work seriously as a part of your devotion to the Lord?

Dissatisfied   1   2   3   4   5   6   7   Satisfied

Not double tongued (1 Timothy 3:8). Are you hypocritical, saying one thing to one person and something contradictory to another?

Dissatisfied   1   2   3   4   5   6   7   Satisfied

As to Things

Not addicted to much wine (1 Timothy 3:8). Are you addicted to anything that is controlling your life or causing a weaker Christian to stumble and sin against God?

Dissatisfied   1   2   3   4   5   6   7   Satisfied

Not fond of sordid gain (1 Timothy 3:8). Are you controlled by the desire for material wealth or do you seek His kingdom and righteousness first?

Dissatisfied   1   2   3   4   5   6   7   Satisfied

As to Family

A husband of one wife (1 Timothy 3:12). Are you a one-woman man? Do you have a good relationship with your wife?

Dissatisfied   1   2   3   4   5   6   7   Satisfied

Good managers of their children and their own households (1 Timothy 3:12). Do your wife and children love, respect, and follow your leadership? Are they responding to God and His claim on their lives?

Dissatisfied   1   2   3   4   5   6   7   Satisfied

Supplement N: *Spiritual Gifts Evaluation*

Score each statement to the extent it reflects your life experience.

3	2	1	0
Much	Some	Little	None

_____ 1. I enjoy planning and organizing.

_____ 2. I am motivated to speak to those who are upset.

_____ 3. I feel a desire to help when confronted with the urgent financial needs of others.

_____ 4. I hurt for those who are, of their own doing, poor, sick, imprisoned, etc.

_____ 5. I readily volunteer to assist others.

_____ 6. I desire to see others understand the Bible.

_____ 7. I accept leadership positions when offered.

_____ 8. I am sensitive and sympathetic to the discouraged.

_____ 9. I willingly maintain a lower standard of living in order to meet the needs of others.

_____ 10. I have performed acts of love and kindness for those who couldn't, or I knew wouldn't, return them.

_____ 11. I would rather be supportive in the background than highly visible.

_____ 12. I enjoy discovering the meaning of biblical truths and sharing what I've learned.

_____ 13. I am able to organize ideas, people, things and time effectively.

_____ 14. I willingly offer advice to those who desire it.

_____ 15. I consider all that I have to be at God's disposal.

_____ 16. I am content to serve the suffering and undeserving.

_____ 17. I allow others to be in charge while I assist.

_____ 18. When listening to a teacher, I often think of different ways to convey the same information.

_____ 19. I enjoy setting goals and making plans to achieve them.

_____ 20. I attempt to console the broken-hearted and bereaved.

_____ 21. I give liberally to the Lord's work.

_____ 22. I enjoy hospital and/or nursing home visitation.

_____ 23. I am content performing jobs considered unimportant by other people.

_____ 24. I greatly desire to relate biblical truth to life.

_____ 25. I am able to inspire others to achieve a group goal.

_____ 26. I verbally encourage those who are depressed.

_____ 27. I can give cheerfully and not miss what I've given.

_____ 28. I enjoy working with mentally or physically handicapped persons.

_____ 29. I enjoy performing a task that requires much effort, but garners little thanks or recognition.

_____ 30. I enjoy teaching or have enjoyed teaching a Sunday school class.

_____ 31. I effectively delegate responsibility rather than doing everything myself.

_____ 32. I express my love for God through sacrificial giving or sacrificial effort.

_____ 33. I enjoy or have enjoyed holding a church office that is necessary, but not overly important.

_____ 34. I often assume responsibility when no official leaders are designated.

_____ 35. I am comfortable encouraging others to be more faithful.

_____ 36. I give to others even when I have little to spare.

_____ 37. I overlook the faults of others and lovingly accept them.

_____ 38. I have communicated biblical truths to others that have been a help to them.

_____ 39. I have taken opportunities to counsel the troubled.

_____ 40. I am able to talk cheerfully with those who are lonely, ill, shut-in, etc.

_____ 41. I give the credit to others even though I have helped.

_____ 42. I seek to gain understanding of difficult biblical passages and help others understand them.

Key for Spiritual Gifts Evaluation

Insert the score you gave yourself for each question. Total each line, giving you a score for each gift.

Gift	Corresponding Questions							Total
Administration	1_____	7_____	13_____	19_____	25_____	31_____	34_____	_____
Exhortation	2_____	8_____	14_____	20_____	26_____	35_____	39_____	_____
Giving	3_____	9_____	15_____	21_____	27_____	32_____	36_____	_____
Mercy	4_____	10_____	16_____	22_____	28_____	37_____	40_____	_____
Helps	5_____	11_____	17_____	23_____	29_____	33_____	41_____	_____
Teaching	6_____	12_____	18_____	24_____	30_____	38_____	42_____	_____

A total of 18–21 indicates a gift is very likely. Focus your ministry here.

A total of 14–17 indicates a gift is likely. Focus on this area and look for others to confirm it.

A total of 10–13 indicates a gift is possible. Experiment in this area and note if others confirm it.

A total below 10 indicates a gift is doubtful. Seek to minister in other areas.

Supplement O: Church Restoration and Discipline

I. Reasons for Restoration

    A. To cause a return to a biblical standard of conduct and doctrine in a member who errs (Galatians 6:1).

    B. To maintain purity in the local church (1 Corinthians 5:6).

    C. To deter others from sinning (1 Timothy 5:20).

II. Restoration Procedure (Matthew 18:15-18)

    A. Any member of the church who has knowledge of an erring member's false teaching or misconduct shall first attempt to correct the erring member privately, seeking his/her repentance.

    B. If the erring member does not heed the warning, the warning member shall go back to the erring member accompanied by one or two witnesses to warn again and correct the erring member, seeking his/her repentance.

    C. If the erring member still refuses to listen and repent, then the matter shall be brought to the attention of the elders.

    D. After careful and prayerful investigation, the elders shall warn the erring member and tell the matter to the church.

    E. If the erring member refuses to heed the warning of the elders and the church, he/she shall be publicly dismissed from the church.

III. Reinstatement After Restoration

    A. If the erring member eventually heeds the warnings and demonstrates repentance, he/she may request reinstatement to membership.

    B. He/she will be publicly restored to membership and welcomed back into the fellowship of the church.

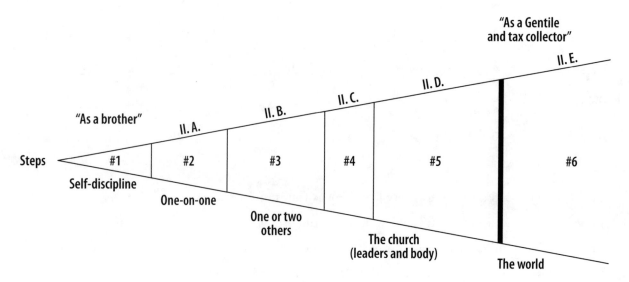

*From Jay Adams' *Handbook of Church Discipline.*

Managing Conflict in the Church

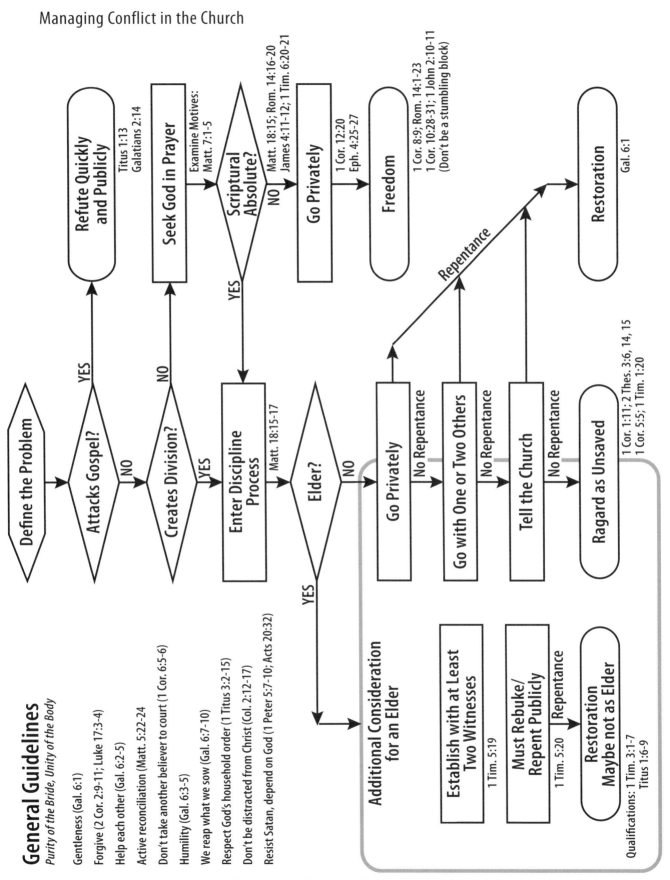

General Guidelines
Purity of the Bride, Unity of the Body

Gentleness (Gal. 6:1)

Forgive (2 Cor. 2:9-11; Luke 17:3-4)

Help each other (Gal. 6:2-5)

Active reconciliation (Matt. 5:22-24)

Don't take another believer to court (1 Cor. 6:5-6)

Humility (Gal. 6:3-5)

We reap what we sow (Gal. 6:7-10)

Respect God's household order (1 Titus 3:2-15)

Don't be distracted from Christ (Col. 2:12-17)

Resist Satan, depend on God (1 Peter 5:7-10; Acts 20:32)

Updated from the work of Glen Vonk, Elder, Fellowship Bible Church, Fuquay-Varina, North Carolina, USA.

Supplement P: *Process for Starting New Churches*

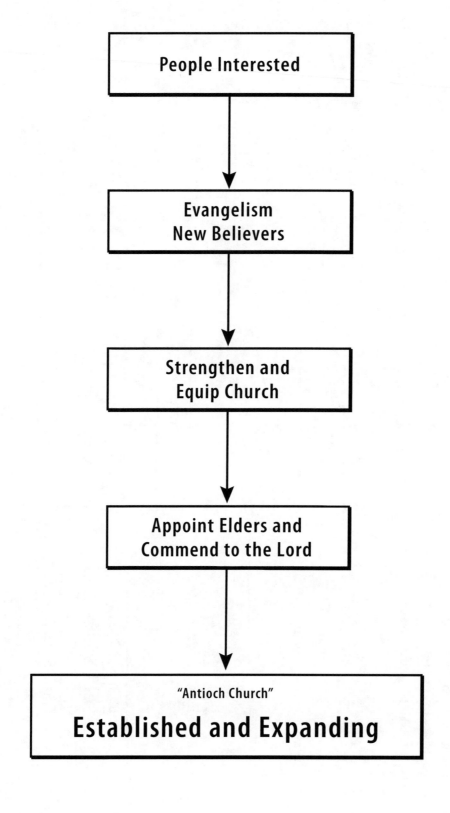

People Interested

↓

Evangelism
New Believers

↓

Strengthen and
Equip Church

↓

Appoint Elders and
Commend to the Lord

↓

"Antioch Church"

Established and Expanding

Supplement Q: *Process for Strengthening Existing Churches*

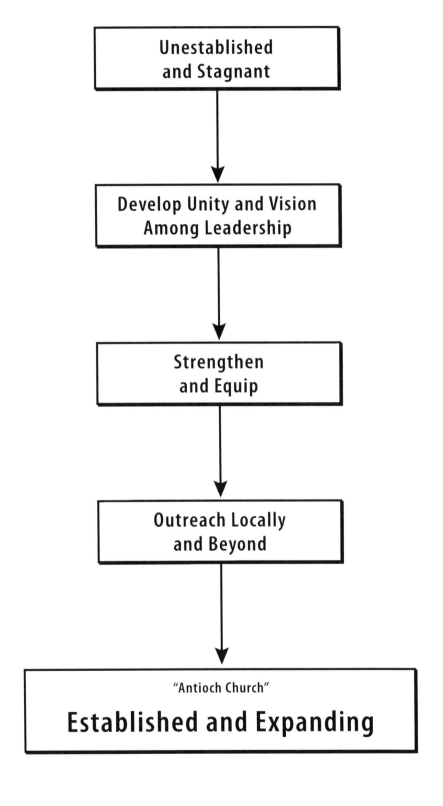

Unestablished
and Stagnant

↓

Develop Unity and Vision
Among Leadership

↓

Strengthen
and Equip

↓

Outreach Locally
and Beyond

↓

"Antioch Church"
Established and Expanding

Progress Record for Lessons and Projects

Session Number	Date Completed	Page(s)	Lesson/ Project	Comments/Action Steps
1		11-17	Reading	
2		21-22	Reading	
3		23	Lesson 1	
4		24	Lesson 2	
5		25	Lesson 3	
6		26	Lesson 4	
7		27	Lesson 5	
8		28	Lesson 6	
9		30-31	Project A	
10		32	Lesson 7	
11		33	Lesson 8	
12		34	Lesson 9	
13		35-36	Project B	
14		37-39	Reading and Project C	
15		41-42	Reading and Project D	
16		45-47	Reading and Section #1	

Session Number	Date Completed	Page(s)	Lesson/ Project	Comments/Action Steps
17		47-48	Section 2	
18		48-49	Section 3	
19		49-51	Section 4	
20		51-52	Section 5	
21		53	Project E	
22		57-59	Reading and Lesson 10	
23		60	Lesson 11	
24		61	Lesson 12	
25		62	Lesson 13	
26		63	Project F	
27		64	Lesson 14	
28		65	Project G	
29		69-71	Reading and Lesson 15	
30		72	Lesson 16	
31		73	Lesson 17	
32		74	Lesson 18	

Session Number	Date Completed	Page(s)	Lesson/ Project	Comments/Action Steps
33		75	Lesson 19	
34		76	Lesson 20	
35		77	Lesson 21	
36		78	Lesson 22	
37		79	Project H	
38		81	Lesson 23	
39		82	Lesson 24	
40		83	Lesson 25	
41		84	Lesson 26	
42		85	Lesson 27	
43		86	Lesson 28	
44		87	Lesson 29	
45		88	Lesson 30	
46		89	Project I	
47		90	Lesson 31	
48		91	Lesson 32	

Session Number	Date Completed	Page(s)	Lesson/ Project	Comments/Action Steps
49		92	Lesson 33	
50		93	Lesson 34	
51		94	Lesson 35	
52		95	Lesson 36	
53		96	Lesson 37	
54		97	Lesson 38	
55		98	Lesson 39	
56		99	Lesson 40	
57		100	Lesson 41	
58		101	Lesson 42	
59		102	Project J	
60		105-108	Project K	
61		109	Project L	
62		110	Project M	
63		111-112	Profile and Evaluation	

Recommended Resources

Becoming a Titus 2 Woman; A Bible Study. Martha Peace. Focus Publishing. 1997.

Biblical Eldership: An Urgent Call to Restore Biblical Church Leadership. Alexander Strauch. Lewis & Roth Publishers. 1995.

The Study Guide to Biblical Eldership. Alexander Strauch. Lewis & Roth Publishers. 1997.

Church Planting Movements: How God is Redeeming a Lost World. David Garrison. Wigtake Resources 2003

Communicating Christ Cross-Culturally. David J. Hesselgrave. Zondervan. 1991.

Different by Design. John MacArthur. Chariot Victor Publishing. 1994.

Don't Waste Your Life. John Piper. Crossway Books. 2003.

Dynamic Spiritual Leadership: Leading Like Paul. J. Oswald Sanders. Discovery House Publishers. 1999.

The Excellent Wife: A Biblical Perspective. Martha Peace. Focus Publishing. 1999.

The Exemplary Husband: A Biblical Perspective. Stuart Scott. Focus Publishing. 2002.

Experiencing God: Knowing and Doing the Will of God. Henry T. Blackaby and Claude V. King. B&H Publishing Group. 2004.

Handbook of Church Discipline: A Right and Privilege of Every Church Member. Jay E. Adams. Zondervan. 1986.

Let the Nations Be Glad! John Piper. Baker Academic. 2003.

Meetings That Work: A Guide to Effective Elders' Meetings. Alexander Strauch. Lewis & Roth Publishers. 2001.

Men and Women, Equal Yet Different. Alexander Strauch Lewis & Roth. 1999.

Missionary Methods: St. Paul's or Ours? Roland Allen. Wm. B. Eerdmans Publishing Company. 1962.

The New Testament Deacon: The Church's Minister of Mercy. Alexander Strauch. Lewis & Roth Publishers. 1992.

New Testament Deacon Study. Alexander Strauch Lewis & Roth. 1995

Our Sufficiency in Christ. John MacArthur. Word Publishing. 1991.

Planting Churches Cross-Culturally: North America and Beyond. David J. Hesselgrave, Baker Academic. 2000.

Sharpening the Focus of the Church. Gene A. Getz. Victor Books. 1984.

Successful Christian Parenting. John MacArthur. Thomas Nelson. 1999.

Worship in the Early Church. Ralph P. Martin. Wm. B. Eerdmans Publishing Company. 1975.